On Trial in Italy

for Preaching the Bible

Howard Bybee

James Kay Publishing

Tulsa, Oklahoma

On Trial in Italy
for Preaching the Bible
ISBN 978-1-943245-08-6

www.jameskaypublishing.com

e-mail: sales@jameskaypublishing.com

© 2016 Howard Bybee
I have endeavored to recreate events, locations, & conversations
from my present recollection of them.

Cover design by JKP
Author Photo by Kyle Bybee

All rights reserved.
No part of this book may be reproduced in any form or by any means
- except for brief quotations -
without permission in writing from the author.

Dedication

I want to dedicate this book to the person who helped me most during the last sixty-three years, who encouraged me and influenced me to do my best while at the same time looking to the Lord for strength and guidance. You have probably already guessed that I am talking about my wife, Doris. As you read through my autobiography you will learn that she was a small town girl. At least it was a small town when we met in Garland, Texas. Now, its city limit overlaps with the city limit of Dallas.

I say this so you will understand what an enormous decision she had to make when I asked her to marry me. I had done three years of mission work in Italy and was preparing to return to that mission. So, she was not only marrying and leaving home, she was marrying and going half way around the world. I am thankful to the Lord that she took the challenge and became for me, as the Lord said of Eve, "A helper suitable for him." I needed such a helper and am thankful to this day that she filled that role beautifully.

She adjusted to a new husband, a new country, a new language and culture. She fit in beautifully. She learned the language and was by my side helping tremendously during those twenty-five years in Italy. She gave me three beautiful children that have themselves become servants of the Lord. My love for her has continued to grow and will last until the Lord calls us home.

Table of Contents

Preface: The Bloody Cornbread 1
As Far Back as I Can Remember 3
School 11
We Moved 13
We Moved Again 23
Another and Even Greater Move 27
World War II - Duty Calls 31
College Years 37
Answering the Lord's Call 41
Persecution 45
The Baptism of Two Catholic Priests 47
Life Changing Trip to the States 51
Two Missionaries with New Wives Back to Italy 57
The First Public Meeting in Padova 63
Police Disrupt Church Service in Leghorn 67
Back to the States for a While 71
Our Return to Italy in 1958 73
A New Son and a Summons to Be Put on Trial 79
Another Trip Home on a Shoestring 85
Back to Italy Again 87
A Two Year Mission Program for High School Graduates 95
The Lord Pointed us in Another Direction 101
A New Dream Realized 105
Back to Italy Again 111
A New Program is Born or I Might Say Revived & Upgraded 115
An Exciting Development in Our Search for a New Director 117
A 2,300 Mile Trip Through Italy 123
Our Children's Careers 127
A Drastic Change in Our Lives 129
The End - With a Spiritual Postscript 132

PREFACE

THE BLOODY CORNBREAD

"That is the worst looking cornbread I have ever seen!" I thought to myself. We were living and doing mission work in Vicenza, Italy. I had baptized a man who was a barber. He was very faithful and tried to interest his family members. In fact, he succeeded in getting his older brother, Valente, interested in a Bible study. Valente worked a small farm way out in the country. In the process of his study of the Bible he said that there was a situation that he would like to clarify before accepting the Gospel. He then related a strange thing that occasionally happened when they made their daily portion of polenta, a kind of corn meal mush. They made it thick enough that they could pour it onto a board or table and it sets a little, at least enough to slice. They made it in the evening and it was ready to eat the next day. Valente said that occasionally, maybe not more than once or twice a year when they would start to eat the polenta they would notice red streaks running through it that almost looked like blood.

He said that the local Catholic priest told the people that when this happened it was a sign of sin in that house and the way to keep it from continuing to happen was to make a donation to his church. People would make their donations and it would eventually cease happening. I told Valenti that was a very understandable concern on his part. I told him to give me a call just as soon as it happened again. A few weeks went by and one day he called and said the phenomenon had returned the week before but since he did not have a telephone he was not able to call me right away but that he had put some aside. I told him to save it and I would come out the next day. Sure enough he was not exaggerating. The veins running through the polenta really did look like blood. I took the bloody polenta and headed home. By then it was late evening. When I went in I showed it to Doris. When she saw it she said, "You are not going to leave that disgusting looking stuff in my kitchen are you?" She said she could see it multiplying all over the place. Early the next morning I went down to the city laboratory. The moment I took it in the lady said, "I am sure I know what you want to know." She said that she had been aware of that particular phenomenon for several years. She then explained that it was due to a virus in the corn and that the people out in the country ground their own corn and it was not pasteurized. The virus when left in the cornmeal would activate in the polenta and spread only when the temperature and the humidity were both at a precise level, which happened rarely. When I explained this to Valenti he was ecstatic and ready immediately to be baptized. I relate this story because of the integral part Italy has played in my life as you will see shortly. But now, let's start from the beginning.

ON TRIAL IN ITALY for Preaching the Bible

AS FAR BACK AS I CAN REMEMBER

I remember living on a farm in far southwestern Oklahoma. The two towns in the area large enough to be known were Hollis and Altus, about thirty-two miles apart. Between these two towns was Duke, about twelve miles west of Altus, then Gould about eleven more miles west of Duke. Between Duke and Gould was a place called McQueen: a filling station, a store, a one room schoolhouse, and a post office. The tenant farm we lived on was five miles south of McQueen.

The house was a wooden house with three rooms downstairs: a small kitchen with a propane gas stove to cook on and a table to eat on, a living room with a pot-bellied coal stove for heat, and one bedroom.  Upstairs was an unfinished attic with only a floor and the pitched rafters. There were two divided sleeping areas up there. This is where everyone except poppa and momma slept. The toilet was an outhouse about thirty yards from our house.

That leads me to explain an early problem. I was an occasional bed wetter until I was three or four years old. Sometimes my older brother Jay would wake me up in the middle of the night and make me go to the open window and relieve myself. Even a little later, I still had to get up during the night.

Howard Bybee

When I was in the first grade I made friends with a class mate who was from what I thought was a rich family. I am sure they weren't rich but compared to what we had, it seemed so to me. Anyway, once he invited me to go home with him to spend the night. I was delighted. However during the wee hours of the morning I badly needed to go to the bathroom. Everything was dark, it was a strange house and I had to just feel my way. I kept getting more and more miserable but I was determined not to do anything embarrassing so I kept going. By the time I reached the bathroom and found the commode I was about ready to explode.

Our only water supply at home was a cistern (a well, dug by hand and lined on the inside with concrete) that caught the water in gutters that came off the house funneling the water to the cistern when it rained. Naturally the water would get very dirty as time went on. When the water was almost gone someone had to be let down with a rope into the well to clean it out. Guess who? Naturally, the youngest and smallest. I did tell you that I was the baby of the family, didn't I? We also had a barn, a cow pen, and a pig pen. We had horses and four or five milk cows.

When I was older I found out that I was born on March 8, 1926, in Bokchito, Oklahoma, a small place a few miles from Durant. When I was one year old our house burned and so we moved to the sharecropper farm south of McQueen that I described before. We raised mostly cotton and wheat and occasionally some corn. We also always had a garden. Dad would put some watermelon seeds in with the cotton seeds as he was planting. That way, when we picked cotton in the fall we would occasionally come up on a watermelon vine, break open a watermelon and pig out with our hands. What a treat!

My earliest memories are when I was probably three or four years old. I barely remember my mother. I learned later that she had some mental problems and often could not function in a normal fashion. She spent some time in an institution. I am sure it was for that reason that I remember little about her. During those early years I remember my dad and that he was a good man and a hard worker. Emotionally he was very reserved. He was neither affectionate nor expressive but a wonderful man.

this is me

My older brothers, Wayne, Jack, and Tommy were already married and away from home by the time I could remember. Wayne was married and lived in Durant, near where I was born. He was the only one of our family that did not move with us to western Oklahoma when our house in Bokchito burned. He already had a job in a shoe store in Durant. In fact, he married the daughter of the owner of the store. What I remember most about Wayne was his coming occasionally to western Oklahoma to see us and bringing us presents. One of the things he brought us on one occasion was a tennis set, net, rackets and all. We found a fairly level place in the pasture down below our house and enjoyed playing when we were not working in the fields. Wayne's wife, Stella, never came with him. I remember my dad, mother, Harold and I going to see them once at their place in Durant. We never went again. Looking back I can understand why. Stella was the only child of a well-to-do couple. Our family, on the other hand, was dirt poor with patched clothes and resoled shoes. We were not much into neatness and cleanliness or social graces. I remember, in fact, being amazed at Wayne and Stella's indoor plumbing and bathtub. Harold and I took a bath together and had a hilarious time, splashing water everywhere. It is not hard to figure out why we never went back. We were never invited.

Jack had moved to Tracy, California and I don't remember him at all until I was about 14. He, his wife and five year old son, Jack David, came from California to see us. I remember Harold and me laughing at how funny Jack David talked with his California accent. Jack worked as an auto mechanic and eventually became manager of the shop. At only about middle age he had an ulcer to start bleeding while he was away fishing. When he got to the hospital the doctor botched this surgery and Jack died.

I remember Tommy as a married man and we all liked his wife, Ruby. She was also from a poor family. They lived not far from where we lived on the farm south of McQueen, probably about ten miles. Harold and I would ride double on our only bicycle to see them and spend the night. We would put some rags for padding on the bar between the seat and handle bar. Harold would sit on the seat and I would straddle the bar. We would both put our feet on the pedals and away we would go. During those years Tommy worked on the WPA. That stood for Works Progress Administration, a public works program started by Franklin D. Roosevelt to give work and minimum wage to the unemployed. A little later Tommy and Ruby moved to California and got a job with a carnival that went up and down the west coast. He did that until the carnival made a stop in Springfield, Oregon. He found a job there in a plywood plant.

Thelma, the only girl in the family, came next and I do remember her being at home only occasionally because she attended a teacher's College at Cordell, Oklahoma. When she was home during the summer she taught adult night classes at the school we attended, called Lahoma. It was about seven miles from where we lived. I remember going with Thelma occasionally to teach her night school classes. It was at that point that I began to remember her. One of the things I remember most was aggravating her, in fact, I was rather mischievous as a kid. I recall one day I was pestering her and she slapped me really hard across the face. Since I knew that I deserved it I didn't want to act cowardly and cry so in a loud voice, said, "Pow!" Everyone that was in the room laughed and laughed about that. Only after I grew up did I realize what a blessing the little income she received for these night classes was to us. Then she got a job teaching at the Lincoln school down closer to the Red River, about twenty miles from where we lived. She later married one of her students, Bill Corley. When WWII started, Bill joined the navy. He was stationed for quite a while at Treasure Island in the bay between San Francisco and Oakland. While he was there Thelma moved to Tracy, CA, where my brother, Jack, lived. That was a blessing because it was only about fifty miles from Oakland. That way she could occasionally visit Bill and he could visit her.

Since I am not far from my paragraph about being a little rascal I will tell of a joke I played one April Fools' Day. This happened when I was about five years old. Our food consisted of whatever we could get and was very simple: cornbread and beans, beans and cornbread, gravy for breakfast and sometimes eggs. We even made desert by pouring syrup over our cornbread. We kept the syrup in an aluminum pitcher. One April Fools' Day just before we ate I was in the kitchen alone and I poured the syrup out of the pitcher and put water in it. As fate would have it papa was the first to crumble his cornbread in his plate and picked up the pitcher. Naturally with water instead of syrup it was lighter than usual and he thought it was almost empty so he turned it over and filled his plate with water. I was cringing but mustered up enough courage to say, "April Fool!" and everyone laughed, fortunately even Papa.

Now that I have described my family and siblings I will talk about things I remember growing up on the farm south of

McQueen. I worked in the fields almost as far back as I can remember. All during the summer we "chopped cotton". At least that is what we called it meaning we went up and down the rows of cotton that had just sprouted and begun to grow and with a hoe chopped the weeds from around the cotton plants. It was hot tiring work. Before I was even able to wield the hoe I was the water boy, taking water to those working in the field. The day started before daylight. We would go to the barn, milk the cows, feed the hogs, which we called "slopping the hogs". Slop was basically leftover food and table scraps. We would then eat breakfast and go to the field to work. We worked all day taking about an hour for lunch. We quit work while there was still enough daylight to round up the cows from the pasture, milk them, then eat supper.

Sometimes after supper we were able to hear some squeaky, radio programs. We loved to listen to *The Lone Ranger*, or *Lum & Abner*, at the Jot'em down Store. We would also look forward to the broadcast of the heavyweight boxing matches. I remember names like Joe Lewis, Max Schmeling, Primo Carnera, Max Baer, etc. The radio was powered by a car battery and our greatest fear was that the battery would be dead when the fight came on, or worse yet, die before it was over. The battery had to be taken to town to be charged. Bedtime came early because dawn came even earlier, it seemed.

There was occasionally time to play, especially during the winter. We had practically no bought toys. We had to invent and make them ourselves. We would play with old rubber tires. We would just roll them around by hitting them on the top as we ran beside them. Anything round we would use to play with, like a metal rim from an old wooden barrel etc. We would make a paddle by nailing a short crosspiece of wood onto the end of a longer piece. We would get the rim rolling then run along and push it from the back with the paddle.

ON TRIAL IN ITALY for Preaching the Bible

We played a lot of Cowboys and Indians with our homemade guns. We would take an old rubber inner tube, cut it into strips about half an inch wide. This was the ammunition. We then took a piece of wood about three inches long and whittle it until it would fit nicely into a closed fist. Then we would take a longer piece, about ten to twelve inches, make it a little less in diameter than the stock and nail it onto the stock. There was the semblance of a gun. Then we would fasten a clothespin onto the back of the stock. *Voila!* A lethal weapon. We took one of the rubber bands made from the inner tube, pinch one end together, place it in the clothespin and stretch the rubber band until we could put the other end over the end of the barrel. Then we could search and find an Indian (a brother or a neighbor), aim the gun, open the clothespin – dead Indian. When neighbor friends came we would divide up into Cowboys and Indians. One team would go and hide, anywhere around the house, barn, cow pen, or wherever. Then the war was on.

We had usually two or three dogs. Our favorite was the Greyhound. Harold and I would take him rabbit hunting. We would walk with him through the fields and pastures until we jumped a rabbit. Old Red would take out after it and almost always catch it. This was not just fun it was also supper, fried rabbit and gravy, yum. Our brother Wayne also brought Harold and me a BB gun. We had fun shooting birds with it, mostly sparrows. I also remember one Christmas getting a little toy car, a little bigger than matchbox size. I spent hours alone down in the pasture making a road with a knife along the side of a small hill and pushing that car along that road.

SCHOOL

I started to school at six years of age. We were picked up and brought home by a school bus. We had to walk about half a mile to catch the bus and the bus probably went twenty or thirty miles picking up kids. As I mentioned the grade school and high school was called Lahoma and was about five miles from where we lived. I remember quite a bit about the grade school we went to, it had good teachers and good discipline. The discipline was rather convincing, it was usually a slap on the hand with a wooden ruler or for major foul-ups a paddling on the behind with a good sized paddle. I remember some good friends there and especially playing with them during recess. The games were mostly Red Rover, Stealing Sticks, hockey with sticks and a beat up tin can as a puck, etc.

I remember one not too happy incident when I was in the second or third grade. A neighbor friend of ours talked Harold and me into running away from school one day and walking home. We made it fine and when we got near home we stopped at a mud tank or pond we had in our lower pasture. We stripped off our clothes, and jumped in. We were playing, swimming, and looking for crawdads (Crayfish). We looked toward the house and saw our dad coming towards us. We got out quickly, put on our clothes and went to meet him. Naturally, he wanted to know why we were not in school. When we told him he didn't like it, he got his discipline tool, a leather razor strap, and started applying it to Harold and me. I distinctly remember crying as loud as I could thinking that if I did, he would have mercy. It really worked, in fact, it wasn't all that bad.

I learned to drive our Model T Ford pickup when I was about eight years old. I also remember once when our brother Tommy came over he took me for a ride around the yard in the pickup. He got to going pretty fast and turned quickly in a circle, my door came open and I went flying out. Thankfully it didn't really hurt me. Later we got a Model A Ford. One thing that stands out in my memory about it happened on a wet muddy day. My brother Jay had driven the Model A to school and they asked him to drive the school bus home. Even though I was only about nine he let me drive the car home. The roads were very muddy and filled with potholes. I somehow had learned that if you approach a mud hole you had better get up enough speed to get through it. I had to do that two or three times that day and was proud of myself that I made it home.

During those years we went almost every Sunday to a church of Christ that met in the one room schoolhouse at McQueen. I remember a lady teaching us kids in one corner of that room while the adults used the other part for their Bible study. I also remember going occasionally to brush arbor (so called) gospel meetings. By the time we started going they had started using a large canvas tent. The lighting was kerosene lanterns and did they ever attract the bugs. I was happy if I could lean over onto someone and go to sleep. They just usually carried me home and put me to bed.

ON TRIAL IN ITALY for Preaching the Bible

WE MOVED

Everything was pretty normal during those years. Then we moved farther down into the corner of Oklahoma. The Texas-Oklahoma state line was to the west of our farm and the Red River the southern boundary. The nearest school and post office was called Bethel. We had a few horses and a few cows and, of course, some farm equipment. Our mother had come back from a home for mentally troubled people and was doing what she could at home. One day not long after we had moved there my dad came to find me and told me that our mother had drunk some lye and had to be taken to the hospital. Shortly thereafter I was taken to the hospital but was not taken into her room. I waited in the hallway as people went in and out then they came out and told me that she had died. She was taken for burial to the Lahoma graveyard. Before the funeral her body was taken to our friends home, the Bradfords, just two or three miles from where we previously lived. There are only a couple of things that stand out in my memory about that event. We stayed with the Bradfords during that time and the thing I remember most clearly is that their boys and Harold and I played out behind the barn while the visitation was going on. Then the next day the kids in my grade at school were brought to the little chapel at the cemetery for the funeral. That made an impression on me.

Life went more or less back to normal down on the farm. I know it was hard for my dad to do all the farm work and also cook and keep house. However, I don't remember ever going hungry or feeling neglected. Then about five or six months later a bombshell exploded, figuratively speaking. My dad told us that he had to go to Oklahoma City, about three hundred miles away, which seemed to us then like going to New York. He did not tell us why he was going. When he came back he had a new wife and step daughter, Emma and Eileen. To me it was not a big deal, kind of like he had bought a new horse or something. Then the fireworks started. My sister, Thelma, and a couple of my brothers came down and berated my dad for acting so secretly and foolishly. Thelma had been very close to my mother and had often cared for her. She thought that Dad's actions were disrespectful and that he remarried much too soon. We then learned that Dad had found out about Emma through an ad in the Oklahoma City newspaper, a lady wanting to find a husband. That night, when my sister and some of my brothers came, a scene stands out in my memory. It was already dusk and I walked up and down a treelined road beside our house and down the road a ways I could hear Thelma and the others sobbing and lamenting. You can imagine what kind of impression that reception made on Emma. She was by nature a belligerent and foul mouth person. This started her off on a very sour note.

After a while life did get back to some kind of normalcy, at least into a routine. Emma was very harsh with her daughter, who was about four years younger than me. One of the extreme things she did occasionally was to paddle Eileen with the flat side of a butcher knife. On the plus side, however, she did her work. She cooked pretty well and cleaned, after a fashion. At least she kept us all going. We had about one section of land that we worked. My chores became a little more involved. I began driving two horses pulling a cultivator or a knife sled down the rows in the fields. You probably know what a cultivator is but probably not a knife sled. It was made with two 2 x 10 boards about seven foot long. A slant was cut in the front of the two boards to make it sled like. They were then nailed together about eight inches apart. Two large knife type blades were fastened to the outside slanting backwards. The front side of the blades was sharp. It also had a seat on it. We would hitch two horses to it that would pull it down the furrow where the cotton had been planted and sprouted. The sled would fit pretty well on both sides of the young cotton plants and the blades would cut about six inches under the mounds on either side of the cotton rows. This naturally cut the weeds from the cotton rows. The sled also had one other feature. Onto the very back of the sled two metal hooks were attached that would barely loosen the dirt close to and on either side of the cotton plants. This would give the plants a better chance to grow.

I went into this detail in order to tell this story. We had three horses and a mule. One of the horses was very gentle "old Maude" we called her. We kids would jump on her at any time with no saddle and sometimes no bridle just for fun. One of the other horses was very skittish and you would never know whether or not she would stay in the traces. One day I was far down in the field sledding the cotton rows with this horse and another one. The hooks on the back of the sled would unfortunately gather lose tumble weeds. Sometimes to the degree that it would impede what they were supposed to be doing. I would have to stop, get off, go back and dig the weeds from the hooks. Once it happened that while I was back digging the weeds out from the hooks the unruly horse got spooked and naturally the other one followed suit. Away they went and lo and behold one of the hooks had found its way through the suspender of my overalls. As a result I was dragged behind as the horses and sled headed straight for the barn over terraces and whatever. Fortunately after a short while my suspender broke and I lay on the ground watching the flying, bouncing, flipping sled. As I had hoped when the horses reached the barn they stopped, still hooked to what was left of a mangled sled.

I sometimes road this horse to our mailbox, a mile and a quarter from our house. On one occasion she did her thing again and I had to hang on for dear life as she ran full speed all the way back home. That is what we called "special delivery". While I am wondering how I made it through those years I might mention another incident or two. One relates to rattlesnake encounters. These were many, even finding them in our cellar where we kept food often in jars that needed a cooler place. One cold winter day I was out on the back forty fixing a broken fence. The post had not only fallen but I couldn't even find it. I looked around and found what appeared to be the post. As I picked it up I realized that it was a rattlesnake.

Fortunately the weather was below freezing and the snake had frozen stiff. I did, though, let it go very quickly. I might mention another rather dangerous incident but this one was by choice. The Red River, as I mentioned ran along the southern side of our farm. The water in it usually was rather low and not very fast except when floods came. Once, a rather strong rain storm caused the river to rise even beyond its banks. Harold and I were down watching it and Harold dared me to swim across it. At that age you do not turn down a dare so I took my clothes off and jumped in. I had to huff and puff but finally made it over. However, by the time I reached the other side I was half a mile downstream. As is obvious, someone up there was watching after me.

Life with Emma was a challenge but I accepted the status quo and eventually gained her favor. I was the only one of the Bybee clan that she ever cared for. I mentioned earlier some of my rascal (prank) qualities and I never did lose those. Once, in fact, on Halloween I had to be a little inventive to have some fun. I am not sure where Harold and Jay were but I was the only one home with Dad and Emma. Our nearest neighbor was about a mile away and to get there we would have to go through a rather rocky pasture with a few trees and mostly

ON TRIAL IN ITALY for Preaching the Bible

bushes. I decided to make me a Halloween costume and go to our neighbors to celebrate and play with these friends. I wrapped a bunch of rags around the straw part of a broom; put a mask and a hat on it and a sheet just under the head for me to stand under. When I got to our neighbors all was dark and my friends were not home. I made my way back home. As I approached our house I could tell that Emma was in the kitchen at the sink washing dishes. By then it was dark. I also knew that just in front of the sink is a small kitchen window. Never able to skip such an opportunity, I snuck up to the outside of that window, held the masked image up in front of the window and knocked on the wall. Talk about someone being scared to death, it almost happened.

Life down on that farm during those years was not easy. However, I did not know it because I had nothing to compare it with. These years were during the Dust Bowl times in western Oklahoma. When I say "dust" I learned well what that is. Not only was there little rain and everything was dry but there were also occasionally dust storms. These were odd phenomenon. We could see the dust storm approaching from miles away. It looked like a huge dark cloud on the horizon. When it would hit the wind was strong and the dust in the air so thick that you could hardly see your hand in front of your face. It would sting the skin if you stayed out in it. After it passed we had to start cleaning the dust from inside the house. In fact, we had to use shovels to get it out before using the brooms.

I mentioned earlier that when we lived south of McQueen. Dad would take us all to church on Sunday. For some reason, that I never learned, after we moved down near Bethel Dad never went to church. As I said before, Dad was very non-communicative. I remember that during that time someone gave me a small New Testament and I told them that I would read it, try to learn it, and follow it. Harold and I started attending a small Baptist group in Bethel. Once we went when they were having a revival meeting. At the end of each sermon they would have an invitation plea that went on for quite a while. During that invitation plea some of the women went around to people pleading for them to come, as they said, to the Lord. They also made this plea to Harold and me and we went forward and were what they called "saved". About a month later they announced that they were having a baptismal service. They took about five of us to the nearby creek and baptized us.

Life on the farm near Bethel was rather routine: up before sunup, livestock chores, breakfast and either to the field to work or to school according to the season. When we got home from school we did field work and chores. We then ate upper (as we called it) which was usually cornbread and beans. We had school home work at times, some radio time (the things I mentioned before) then to bed. One other thing that stands out in my memory was playing games while we waited for the school bus in the mornings. I mentioned that our mailbox was almost a mile from our house. Well, that is where we had to go to catch the school bus. Kids from two other families on adjacent farms also came to the same bus stop. Often it was a while before the bus came so we would play. One of our favorite games was "Stealing Sticks". We divided into two teams, drew a long line on the ground then on either side of the line, back about twenty feet or so, we would draw in the dirt a circle about four feet in diameter. We placed the same number of sticks in each circle. Then the two teams stood on the line facing each other. The goal was to run around the opponent and without them touching you reach the circle. If you did so without being touched you were then allowed to take a stick and put it into your circle. If, on the other hand, you were touched before you reached their circle you were put as a prisoner into their circle. If one of your team mates made it safely to the cir-

ON TRIAL IN ITALY for Preaching the Bible

cle they could take you out rather than a stick. Many hours were passed with this ingenious game.

ON TRIAL IN ITALY for Preaching the Bible

WE MOVED AGAIN

After about three years on the Bethel farm we moved again. This time to a sharecropper farm about three miles west of Duke. Remember, the main east west highway in those parts: the town closest to the Texas line was Hollis. Then going east Gould, McQueen, Duke, then Altus. This is for you geography buffs. The first thing that surprised us after we moved there is that on the first Sunday we saw our dad getting dressed up. We asked him where he was going and he said "to church". That really surprised us but since we knew no one there we decided to go with him. When we got to town we went to the church of Christ and we noticed that the Baptist church was just across the street. We decided that we would go with dad until we got somewhat acquainted then we would go to the Baptist church, after all, with that group is where we had been baptized. That day at church we met a couple of boys about our age. We hit it off and after a couple of times Emma agreed that we could invite them to go home with us for lunch. In a short time we struck up a real friendship. One day while playing with them we told them that beginning the next Sunday Harold and I would go to the Baptist church. They asked why and we told them that it was because we had been baptized at a Baptist church. Carol, the older one, asked us why we were baptized. We said that we didn't know except that they told us we should. He opened a pocket New Testament he had and showed us some scriptures that say that baptism is an act of faith, that it washes away our sins and puts us in Christ. In fact, the scripture he showed us was Acts 2:38 that says: *"Peter replied, "Repent and be baptized every one of you, in the name of Jesus Christ for the forgiveness of your sins and you will receive the gift of the Holy Spirit."* He said that one must know that before he is baptized and that he must confess the name of Christ and repent of his sins before being baptized. He said he also knew that the Baptists did not teach that. We then decided that we needed to know more. We continued to attend the church of Christ and study the Bible, especially the topic of conversion. Then in about a month we were immersed for the remission of our sins and understood very well the scriptural reason for it.

Our work load on the new farm was about the same as on the other farms. At one point we got a few sheep and one little goat. We loved to play with the goat. One day the goat got out in the road that passed in front of our house. A passing car hit and killed it. As I said we never had much variety in our meals so my dad butchered it and man was that ever good eating. That pretty well overshadowed the loss. Always we worked in the field chopping cotton, picking cotton, etc. However, there were periods when we would get caught up and Harold and I were allowed to work for a neighbor for a few cents a day. Harold and I saved all that we made through the summer and that fall we decided to buy something. We found a neighbor who had a used, a very used, Model T Ford for sale. He was asking $20 for it and that is exactly what we had saved up. So we were motorized, sometimes, that is, when we could get it to run.

The next year, though, we were able to upgrade. I had enrolled in a vocational class at school and it was auto mechanics. I then ran across a 1936 Ford coupe. The motor in it was shot so I got it for almost nothing. I then took it to the vocational class and the teacher agreed that we would overhaul the motor as a class project. What a happy day when we got it finished. I started it up and it started immediately. But the throttle on the carburetor was not properly adjusted; consequently it was hung on full speed with no way to reduce it. Before we shut it off the piston bearings were ruined. So the class got more practice repairing cars, we had to redo it. We used the old car whenever we could afford to buy gas. After all, it was 15 cents a gallon.

I was in the 10th grade when I entered the Duke public school. I made a number of friends and enjoyed my time there. Other than the automotive class another thing I enjoyed was the physical education period. A part of that class was devoted to boxing. I thought I was pretty good at it in fact I won one of the area wide tournaments. I guess I could say consequently that I was a boxing champion. Maybe I had better explain a little about that though. I was taken along with the other Duke boxer to an area wide tournament. There were only three entered in my category one did not show up and just before my fight the other entry conceded and backed out so I was the winner.

ANOTHER AND EVEN GREATER MOVE
OKLAHOMA TO OREGON

By the time I was in the eleventh grade Dad had begun to see the handwriting on the wall. Through the years past he had a great deal of help with the farm from all my brothers as they grew up. They were, of course by this time long gone. I mentioned before that Tommy and Ruby moved to California and got a job with a carnival that went up and down the west coast. The carnival thing was a terrible job, but it was a job. At one point the carnival stopped at Springfield, Oregon, just across the river from the city of Eugene. Tommy found a job in a sawmill plant so they settled there. By then WWII had started and most of the younger men went away to war. That left businesses like the plywood plant very short handed. Tommy wrote my dad and said, "Why don't you move out here? You can get a job in the plant where I work even though you are in your late fifties." Dad knew that in a very few years Harold and I would both be gone and he would have no help on the farm so he decided to make the move. That meant selling everything we had in the way of equipment, animals, etc. We didn't get much for it all but ended up with more cash than we had ever had. For the trip dad bought a 1939 Chevrolet sedan. It was used but compared to anything we had ever owned, to us it was like a Mercedes.

Finally the day of departure came and dad and I, with Emma and her daughter Eileen, loaded up. Since Harold was in his senior year at school he decided to stay there. One of the teachers agreed to keep him. It was winter time and that contributed to a difficult trip. When we got to Arizona it began to snow. The snow and ice began to build up along and on the side of the road. About ten miles past Flagstaff dad could not see the road well, got onto the side and hit the cement shoulder of a bridge with the front wheel. People in a passing car going the other way stopped and we asked them to please send a wrecker from Flagstaff. The wrecker came and towed us back there. The suspension on the right front was badly damaged. Those '39 Chevrolets had the first crude type of hydraulic suspension. It was during the war and parts were hard to get. We were forced to trade the car for a used 1936 Ford coupe. How sadly we gave up our Mercedes. Since the four of us could not ride in the coupe Emma and Eileen had to go on to Oregon on the train and dad and I took the car.

We made it to Springfield. There we started a different kind of life. We rather quickly found and bought a small house. Dad went to work in the plywood plant and Eileen and I started to school. It was in the middle of my junior year in high school. The thing that stands out the most for me is the way the kids there laughed at how I talked. Oklahoma dialect was very amusing to them. It reminded me of how amused I was years earlier at the California dialect of Jackie, our older brother Jack's son. I guess it was payback for me. I enjoyed the school fine. After I finished the 11th grade the principle told me that I was a little ahead of the others in the class and that I could come to school only half day during my senior year.

That was good news for me and, in fact, I found a job as an auto mechanic helper. It was across the river in Eugene but only about a 30 minute bus ride. The owner of the garage was the only one who worked there. He was a middle aged man, married but with no children. He was really good to work for and taught me a lot. He was very patient as you will understand after I give you an example. We were completely overhauling the motor of a Ford pickup. I took the motor apart and found as was expected that the piston bearings had worn out. I put in new ones and started putting it back together. In the process of dismantling I had to take off the oil pump. Naturally in putting it back on I had to put a new gasket between the pump and the block. Back then you could not buy readymade gaskets, you had to make your own out of a cork type material: make an outline of the opening, cut out the hole for the oil to flow through and the holes for the bolts. I was proud of myself as I put it all back together. Then it came time to try the overhauled motor. It started right up but the boss immediately noticed that there was no oil pressure. He just simply said, "Start taking it back apart until we discover what the problem is." I drained the oil, took off the oil pan then the oil pump. There I checked the gasket I had made and, lo and behold, there were holes for the bolts that held it on but no hole for the oil to pass through. Okay, remedy time, I put it back together and, wow! It worked well.

ON TRIAL IN ITALY for Preaching the Bible

WORLD WAR II - DUTY CALLS

I graduated in 1942 the war was still going on then. As you also know, every male over 18 was drafted into the Army. I knew what was coming so I thought I would prefer the navy and consequently I signed up for it. I was sent to Farragut, Idaho for my basic training. It was definitely thirty days of intense boot camp. I did survive. We were then sent to a base in San Diego, California to wait assignment to a ship. We were all

a little naïve when we got there. The guys already there told us that we would love it because it was a very lax base and they did not impose the rules. We believed them and when the bugle blew reveille the next morning we just turned over and went back to sleep. In about ten minutes a hoard of military police came in and put us all in the brig (that's a naval term for jail). In fact we were given a ten day sentence. However, there were so many of us the brig would not hold us all. They then put us in a cabin near the parade grounds and placed an armed sentry in front of it so we could not get out. However, it wasn't bad at all. We just visited, played cards, checkers, etc. while the others were out cleaning up the parade grounds. After five days the base commander became aware that we were not really being punished so he gave orders that we were to be awakened every two hours during the night and taken outside for muster (roll call). The next day, however, my orders came through to be placed on a ship. The rest of my jail time was forgiven. I was assigned to the USS Roi, a small aircraft carrier. It was one of those they called thirty day wonders because it was a merchant ship that in thirty days they had transformed into an aircraft carrier. The ship was in port for repairs and I was given some training as a radar operator. This is what I did on this ship where I served nine months in the Pacific.

I need here to add some information because it greatly affected my future. While in the Brig (the cottage on the parade ground) I began discussing religion with the guy in the bunk above me. He was a Catholic. During the Bible discussion with him another guy in a nearby bunk began helping me find scriptures. It turned out that he was a member of the church of Christ from Avenal, California. Now back to my time line. It so happens that on the tenth day of our brig sentence Francis, my new friend, was assigned to my same ship. What a blessing! We became best of friends during those months and it was good for both of us. We studied and discussed the Bible quite a bit and both memorized a lot of scriptures

We left San Diego and sailed to San Francisco to pick up fighter planes. My worst fears materialized. I became immediately very seasick and was greatly relieved when we reached San Francisco. I had been told that most sailors usually get sick on their first journey but from then on it's okay. Whoever said that either did not know the facts or did not know me. A few days later our ship headed for Hawaii to deliver the fighter plans. I very quickly realized that I could not walk about on the ship without a bucket in one hand. You can imagine what the bucket was for. After several weeks I finally got to where I did not up chuck on a regular basis unless we got into a storm. However, I never felt completely at ease all the nine months I was aboard the ship except when we were docked. We made several trips from San Francesco to Hawaii delivering fighter planes. Then after a couple of months we started taking planes from Hawaii to the South Pacific islands where the U.S. had naval and air bases.

Life on the high seas was very interesting especially during the war. The things that are the most memorable are the very good and the very bad. Both of these have to do with the weather. Our greatest fear, of course, was encountering a Japanese submarine. Being a radar operator I saw potential danger before anyone, a blip on the radar screen. We had to track the blip on a large Plexiglas display. We radar operators had to learn to write backwards because we wrote on the back side of the Plexiglas screen and the ship's captain could read the large screen from the front and follow the object on the radar. We had those blips come up numerous times but thankfully they always turned out to be some kind of debris, either something another ship had thrown overboard, a tree or log or some remains of a sunken ship. That, in some cases, was scary but the most frightening was something else. Once we were in a storm, a terrible storm. The ship would go way up and way down and from side-to-side. In fact, it would turn so far to one side that even the metal dining tables that were fastened to the floor came loose and slid from side-to-side. If anyone could keep food down during those many hours he had to eat sitting on the floor. Late one night we got into our bunks and tried to sleep. All of a sudden we heard the worst and loudest noise we had ever heard, metal crashing and banging over our heads. We all jumped out of our bunks and headed for the ladder. When we got top side we discovered that the metal barrels of fuel that had been strapped to the bottom of the airplane elevator shaft had broken lose and were being tossed every direction by the storm. That elevator shaft was directly above our sleeping quarters. You can imagine the noise.

That was the worst thing I remember, now for the best. Sometimes the sea was as calm and smooth as glass. It was beautiful and to add to the beauty were the flying fish.

ON TRIAL IN ITALY for Preaching the Bible

We would sit on the front of the flight deck and watch them come zipping out of the water and sail great distances. We would watch them for hours. It is hard to find anything more picturesque than that. We were very blessed that in all the Pacific Ocean that we covered we never did encounter a Japanese submarine nor airplane. There was one airplane exception that I will shortly explain. We spent the last months of the war transporting planes from the Pacific islands all the way to the island of Guam. In fact on one occasion we went to Guam, filled the ship to capacity with fighter planes, and headed toward the American fleet that was at that time just off the coast of Japan getting ready for an invasion. We were going to deliver to them new fighter planes and take on board those that had been damaged or worn out. About half way from Guam to the fleet a Japanese plane flew over but at some distance from us, the first and only enemy craft we had seen. Then within an hour we heard over the radio that the war was over. We celebrated all the way back to Guam. We stayed there several days and even got to go swimming in the ocean while work was being done on our ship. Within a few days, I can't remember exactly how many, they transformed the ship into a troop carrier. They welded bunk beds everywhere. We then went to Tsingtao, China to pick up troops to take back to the U.S. We did get to go ashore for a few hours there in Tsingtao to see a little and buy souvenirs. Fortunately I bought some right away because after a bit my billfold was picked by a thief. So much for my time in China, probably three hours. By then the ship was filled with soldiers and we headed back across the Pacific. At least I can say that I have been to China

ON TRIAL IN ITALY for Preaching the Bible

COLLEGE YEARS

On the way back across the Pacific by ship I thought and talked to Francis a lot about what I would do when I got out of the navy. I had never in my life thought I could ever afford to go to college. Sam, the owner of the auto repair shop where I had worked in Eugene, Oregon had told me as I was leaving for the navy that if I would return there after the war he would let me work for him and eventually inherit his repair shop. Those had been my plans. Francis had a sister that I had met once while on leave from San Francisco. We kinda liked each other and she was planning to go to Pepperdine University. Also Francis had an older brother that had been exempt from the military and was then attending Pepperdine. Francis was also planning to go there. Then came the news concerning the G.I. Bill in which the government offered to pay the college tuition and a stipend to the veterans who wanted to go to college. That made up my mind and I enrolled at Pepperdine.

Life there was good. I declared my major to be Automotive Engineering. Pepperdine had been in existence less than ten years and was like an oasis in the south part of Los Angeles. I will not go into a lot of detail about those next four years but, naturally, things happened that gave direction to the rest of my life. One important thing that happened was my choice of a congregation of the church to attend. Francis and I, and some others who had become my friends, attended the church in Venice (That's California not Italy). It is, in fact, a suburb of Los Angeles. The preacher there started a training class for young men, teaching, among other things, how to prepare and deliver sermons. Then before the semester was up he planned a public gospel meeting and each one of us in the class would preach one night of the meeting. I preached one night and my first sermon was "If I knew I had only one sermon to preach". It is based on the conversion of the Ethiopian Eunuch in Acts chapter 10. I still occasionally preach that sermon. I have an interesting sequel to it that I will tell you about later. I felt good about this first sermon, in fact, so good that I changed my university major from Automotive Engineering to Bible. So as you can see that was quite a change in the direction of my life.

I then began taking more Bible courses as well as public speaking and song leading. Back then preachers often had to do everything. It turns out (that's another way of saying "the Lord was working in my life) that my roommate, Carl Mitchell was also a Bible major. In fact, he was already preaching for a congregation in L.A. I and several other friends began going with him to the Sitchel St. church. Then after a while another Bible Major friend, Bernard Howell, found out that the church out in the California desert town called Barstow needed someone to come preach for them on Sundays. Bernard and I accepted that challenge and took turns going there on Sundays to preach. We would take a car load of fellow students with us each time. Barstow was a small town 115 miles northeast of L.A. We went out to preach at Barstow for about two years. There were many experiences during that time but I will tell you of only two. One was that as we preached there we discovered that there were two Mormon young men also there doing their two year mission. One of them courted and eventually married a young lady from our congregation. Naturally she followed his theology. I learned about the Mormon's two year mission program that required all their young men to give two years to mission work and it planted a seed in my subconscious that eventually, as you will learn later, sprouted and gave my life a new direction. One briefer incident during this period merits a recall. One morning I was making that journey

ON TRIAL IN ITALY for Preaching the Bible

by myself. It was very early Sunday morning and the streets were empty. That tempted me to put my foot a little heavily on the pedal. Then very quickly I saw flashing lights behind me. You guessed it, a highway patrolman. Patrolman, "Where are you going in such a hurry this morning?" Me, "I am going to Barstow to preach for a church." "Oh, is that so? Well, I'll tell you what I will do. If you will promise to preach on obeying the laws of the land I will not give you a ticket." Wow what a relief! That not only saved me money I did not have, but it also gave me a sermon title.

As I mentioned, those four years were great years. I became a member of a club made up mostly of Bible majors called the Tri Phies φφφ. We would meet regularly for Bible discussions and planning benevolent activities. We also competed with other clubs in various sports. One interesting thing about joining the Tri Phi club was their way of initiating new members. The new inductee was blindfolded, driven out into the country and there initiated. This consisted of things like blindfolding the inductee, telling him to open his mouth then one of the members would put a bit of overripe banana onto his finger tip then making the sound in your throat you make when spitting and simultaneously flipping the banana into his mouth. Finally we would pour syrup onto his head along with a little flour and tell him goodbye. He had to walk or hitchhike his was back to the campus.

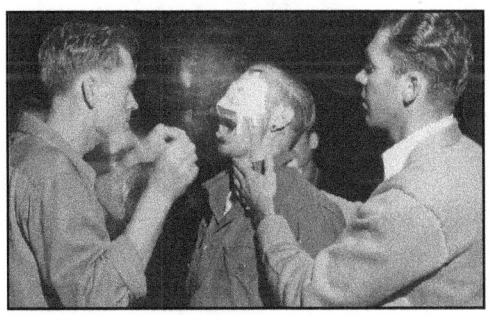

INITIATION INTO THE TRI PHI CLUB IN COLLEGE

ON TRIAL IN ITALY for Preaching the Bible

ANSWERING THE LORD'S CALL

The next phase of my life was influenced by a guy by the name of Harold Paden who attended one semester at Pepperdine in 1948. He talked to Carl and me about plans he had to be part of a team of seven couples who would go to Italy to take the Gospel and that they were leaving the following year, that is, 1949. Harold had been in Italy during the war as a ski trooper. He told us that while there he discovered that the Bible was practically an unknown book. It was unavailable for most people. The people were mostly Catholic at least in name and were not taught to read the Bible. In fact, they were discouraged from reading it even if they found one. Harold said that he told the Lord that if he survived the war he would come back to Italy, bring the Bible, and make it known as much as possible. After the war he convinced his older brother, Cline, to join him and help put together a team. All of this materialized and the team left for Italy early in 1949. They went to Frascati, near Rome, and opened an orphan's home for boys left homeless from the war. Harold and Betty stayed there for about six months

Carl Mitchel and me

then moved to Milano, in northern Italy. He had already started writing Carl and me about all their very interesting experiences, great receptivity among the people but strong opposition from the Catholic Church and consequently from the Police as well. Harold pleaded with us to come to Milano to help them.

That set my course for the next sixty-one years. We left Pepperdine as soon as we graduated and took a Greyhound bus to Abilene, Texas where Carl's parents lived at the time. We then went to Brownfield because the church there had accepted the oversight of the team that had gone and of the orphan's home the team opened in Frascati near Rome. Brother Joe Chisholm, a full time elder, put me in his car and we went up in the Texas panhandle to visit churches and look for commitments of financial help for my support. We returned in about ten days with my support promised, $175 a month. Then Joe took Carl and they went into south Texas. In about the same amount of time they returned with his support arranged and we were set to go. We bought plane tickets for Milano, Italy. We had to make a stopover in Glasgow, Scotland.

Harold and Betty were very happy to see us and Harold explained our living arrangements. Since he had no car and no money to buy one we would live with him and his family for about three months and pay him for our room and board so he could save up money to buy an old car. In fact, Harold found a 1938 Oldsmobile that he bought from some Gypsies for very little. A true Italian would not drive a car that big. It would barely go down some of the narrow streets. It did run though and helped us in our work. Carl and I started studying Italian under a private teacher. Our learning curve was also enhanced by the fact that we were going with Harold to Bible studies with Italians and also spending a lot of time with the Italian Christians. Harold had already taught and baptized about twenty-five people. We were pretty well submerged in the language. I preached my first sermon after we had been there for

ON TRIAL IN ITALY for Preaching the Bible

three months. Of course our language teacher helped me get it presentable and learning a lot of the vocabulary that was necessary. The rest of this story is the shot heard around the world. It has been told and laughed about countless times and countless places. I preached on the conversion of the Ethiopian nobleman of Acts chapter ten. Cornelius in Italian is *"Cornelio"* but there is also a very similar word in Italian *"coniglio"* that sounds pretty much the same. Of course, I pronounced my sermon topic much more like the second word and consequently preached on the conversion of the "rabbit". As I preached I was wondering why the people all had big grins on their faces. I thought as I preached, "That's strange, I haven't told a joke." This has become the most famous language *faux pas* of all the American missionaries. These kinds of funny and embarrassing mistakes are experienced by everyone who learns another language, especially if you do like you should and just launch out even before you are sure you have it all right. In fact, I have a booklet I put together entitled Italian Missionary Bloopers. I will give you a couple of examples from the booklet.

Doris writes: "One day I was at the church office in Vicenza. Luciana Caddeo, the secretary, asked me where Howard was. I wanted to say that he had gone to look for some mimeograph stencils. I thought I knew the word for stencils (which is *matrice* in Italian) so I said: "he has gone to look for some *meratrice*. Luciana said, "Oh, I hope not!", because the word I had used meant 'prostitutes'.

This blooper is from the missionary, Charles Moore. I remember one of Don Shackelford's blunders. He got up after services at Palermo one Sunday to tell the brethren that brother Edwards was going to leave for Naples. 'To leave for' is *partire* but Don, without realizing it, added a few letters and said, *"partorire"*, which means to give birth to. Stretching the point a bit, not only because he is a man but also because Naples had already been born.

Carl stayed in Milano only three months. Then Cline Paden, who was directing the Orphans home near Rome, had to make a trip to the U.S. to raise funds. He asked Carl to replace him while he was gone. I stayed on in Milan for one year. The church continued to grow. We found two small Protestant groups, one in Torino and the other in Alessandria, who had no preacher and asked us if we would preach for them on Sundays. Harold and I took turns, one going to preach for these two groups and the other stayed to preach for the congregation in Milano. We rented a storefront in downtown Milano for the church to meet in. It had a couple of smaller rooms besides the larger one where we had the assembly. I moved down there and lived in one of those rooms.

PERSECUTION

In order to help you understand the following series of events that took me away from Milano I must fill you in on the overall development of the church in Italy. The Catholic Church was in complete control of all things of a religious nature and, for the most part, for political life as well. This was a holdover from the effects of the Lateran Pact. This was an official political pact the Catholic Church made with Mussolini. The Pope made this pact with Mussolini when he and his doctrine called Fascism was gaining power in Italy and was obviously going to win control of the nation. In this pact the Catholic Church promised to support Mussolini and Fascism and help bring it to power if he would make the Catholic Church the only legally recognized church in Italy. Therefore during the period of Fascism the Catholic Church dominated everything of a religious nature and also had great political influence. For many years after the war when Fascism was defeated the Catholic Church still practically controlled the fledgling new government that was developing. It did not want to give up the control they had wielded nor its position as the only church allowed to exist in Italy. Our work of evangelization was very unwelcome to the Catholic leaders and consequently suffered great opposition from them through government leaders and the police. Many of our church buildings were closed by the police, visas were denied, the orphan's home permit was rejected and had to be closed, the priests led youth groups to stone our buildings, and preachers were arrested and put on trial. All of these incidents were reported by the news media both Italian and foreign. Even in the U.S. Life Magazine carried news about this persecution. Always, as we know, the Lord brings good things out of bad and in this case the church of Christ received more publicity than we could have ever dreamed of paying for through the news articles about our persecution.

THE BAPTISM OF TWO CATHOLIC PRIESTS

While I was still in Milano a Catholic priest, Fausto Salvoni, had read in the newspapers about the persecuted church of Christ. He came to us very discontent with Catholic doctrine and a desire to follow only the Bible. Fausto Salvoni had been sent to the seminary to study to become a priest when he was twelve years old. That was customary during the Catholic dominated years of the Mussolini era. The people were very poor and struggled to make a living but if you sent a child to prepare for the priesthood that was an economic advantage for the family.

Fausto was an exceptionally brilliant student. He had managed to obtain a copy of the Bible. He studied it diligently and consequently began to have some doubts about the Catholic doctrine he was being taught. When he expressed these doubts to his confessor at the seminary he was always told not to worry about it because when he became ordained as a priest these doubts would disappear. Naturally that did not happen. He kept rather quiet about these doubts and after being ordained he made a request to be sent to the Catholic university in Rome to study Biblical languages. Because of his exceptional intelligence he was granted that request. While there he learned Greek, Hebrew, and Egyptian hieroglyphics. After finishing the university he was transferred to Milano to teach in the Gregorian Seminary there training priests. He maintained his interest in and belief in the Bible. He thought that he could possibly teach a great deal of Biblical truth to his students without his superiors realizing it. However, word kept getting to his presiding Bishop and Fausto was severely reprimanded many times for what he was teaching.

One day a student asked him if he believed the Catholic tradition concerning the "house of Loreto". That is the house in the small village of Loreto, Italy that the Catholic Church teaches is the house in which Mary conceived Jesus in Palestine. They claim that the house was transported by angles to Loreto, Italy December 10, 1294. It is said to be the most visited holy Catholic site for pilgrims in the world. Fausto told the students that he was certain the tradition was not true because he had seen archeological studies showing that the construction and materials of which the house was made were Italian not Palestinian. Word of Fausto's answer reached the Bishop and he called Fausto to his office. He not only reprimanded Fausto for the way he answered the student's question but told Fausto he was writing the Pope about what Fausto had told the student concerning the house of Loreto. Then a couple of weeks later called Fausto into his office and showed him a letter he had received from the Pope, Pious XII. The letter read: "It does not really matter that there is not absolute proof of the validity of this tradition but the church receives so many spiritual and material blessings from it that it is best to let people believe it." That was the last straw for Fausto. He resigned his position and left the priesthood. He knew he would have a difficult time making a living because ex-priests were shunned by almost everyone and it was against the law in Italy for an employer to hire an ex-priest for any business that had contact with the public. Because of his knowledge of languages, French, German, Spanish, and English, he made an income translating from his home for international businesses. Even these international businesses would not hire Fausto officially nor allow him to work on their premises because of fear of the local Bishop. He had to do his translation work at his home and take it regularly to the businesses.

ON TRIAL IN ITALY for Preaching the Bible

Fausto read in the newspaper about this new religious group in Italy that was being harassed by the Italian police. He read that it was reported to be a Bible based religion so he set about to find the church of Christ. He did find us by talking one day to a man on the streetcar. The man said he had seen a building with a sign on it that said *Chiesa di Cristo* (Church of Christ). With that information Fausto found us. He came and told us his story. He said that he would like to study the Bible with us. Brother Harold Paden studied with him for about a month. Then while studying the New Testament conversion process he said that he wanted to be baptized by immersion. He was baptized and he became a member of the Milano congregation. He began almost immediately to preach. He was an excellent preacher and evangelist.

About two months later early one Sunday morning in the late spring of 1952 the doorbell rang at the church apartment in Milano where I slept so I went to the door. There was a man who asked if this was where the church of Christ met. He then said that he had read in the newspapers about this church of Christ and in one article had read that the group claimed to follow only the Bible. That, he said is what he would like to talk with me about.

That Sunday it was my turn to go to Torino and Alessandria to preach so I just asked him to come with me in the car and we would talk as we went along. He told me that he was an ex-Catholic priest and that he had left the Catholic Church some years before because he became convinced that it's teaching and practices did not conform to the Bible message. As we drove along and discussed the Bible and biblical teachings it became very apparent that he had a good knowledge of the Bible. We arrived in Torino and had our worship and preaching service with that group. We then headed on for Alessandria. As we went along we began talking about what THE New Testament says about how a person becomes a Christian and the scriptural teachings related to it. He immediately said that he had been convinced for some time that a penitent believer should be immersed in baptism for the forgiveness of sins but that he had never found anyone who would baptize him. About that time on our journey we passed over the Po River. I stopped the car, we went down to the river and I baptized Raffaello. We went on to worship with the group in Alessandria and then back to Milano. He told Harold and me that there was a group of about 15 people in Padova that he met and studied the Bible with regularly. He pleaded with us to send someone to Padova to begin the Lord's church. The only ones available were Harold and me and naturally the lot fell on me because Harold was so involved with the work in Milano. Shortly thereafter I moved to Padova. I met with the group Raffaello had mentioned and twelve of the fifteen of his friends were soon baptized into Christ and the church began to meet. Raffaello worked with me and helped in preaching and teaching for the Padova church. The work continued to go well. We started renting a place to meet. The best solution seemed to be an apartment with a good size living room. This worked okay but had its problems. Usually the owners began getting pressure from the local priest for renting to what they called a Protestant group and after the first year's contract expired they would force us to move. We were able to find other apartments to rent but realized that having to move from one place to another adversely affected the stability of the church. After I had been in Padova almost two years I decided to make a trip to the States to inform churches of the work in Italy and hopefully raise funds to buy a building.

ON TRIAL IN ITALY for Preaching the Bible

LIFE CHANGING TRIP TO THE STATES

Interestingly my friend Carl made similar plans close to the same time. I decided that I would start with a visit to my *alma mater*. While visiting friends at Pepperdine I started looking for an old car I might purchase to make my tour of churches. Someone told me that there was a guy there in school that pulled cars from Texas to sell in California to make money for his schooling. I looked him up and found him, Paul Buhler, in the married student apartments. Sure enough he had a five year old Hudson that he sold me at a good price. As we started doing the paperwork he suggested that since I would keep the car only a few months we could save money by leaving it in his name. I was always for anything that saved money. I left there and drove up to Manteca, CA where my sister lived. I visited with her and her family for several days then decided to drive to Abilene, TX where the annual church lectureship was about to begin. I thought it might be a good idea to get some car insurance for my upcoming travels but ran into a problem. The agent told me that I could not buy insurance with the car in someone else's name. I began making phone calls to track down Paul in order to remedy the situation. I found out that he had returned to his home town of Garland, Texas and was staying with his wife, Marge's, parents. When I reached him I told Paul that I was headed to the Abilene lectureship and that afterwards I would come by Garland and we would work out the title/insurance problem.

Off I went then to Abilene. At that time, what with all the problems and persecution the work in Italy was encountering and the publicity it was receiving in the States that was the number one topic at the lectureship. Cline Paden was one of the main speakers. There were quite a number of Italian missionaries there. We met together often, discussed the work, prayed and enjoyed each other's company. Those were interesting times. I then went on to Garland, worked out the car papers with Paul and found out that Marge had a sister, an unmarried sister, in fact. She was a beautiful young lady and I decided right then that I needed to spend some time in the Garland/Dallas area and speak to the churches there. I did so, speaking somewhere in that area three to five times a week. Doris usually consented to go with me and we got more and more acquainted. In fact, during those trips I taught her an Italian song. It was a little ditty called *"Lo Sai Che I Papaveri"* (Do You Know that the Poppies). It is about a little duck that fell in love with a poppy, a very profound song. She learned it well even though she did not know Italian.

    I stayed in that area a couple of months and raised quite a bit of money toward a building for the work in Padova. Then I had to go to Houston for some speaking appointments. Before I left I began thinking that the Lord was leading me to the one who could fill the void in my life. The night before I left for Houston I asked her to marry me and go back to Italy with me. You can imagine what a quandary that put her in even though her positive feelings for me were growing. She said, as anyone would expect under the circumstances, "This is too soon, we don't even know each other." She knew that I was totally dedicated to the growth and spread of the church in Italy. She and I both knew that during those years missionaries came home only once every three years. That's the way it was back then because funds were scarce and travel was expensive. She was torn between a growing affection, the desire to be directly involved in the great commission on the one hand and all the common sense things she had learned about picking a mate for life on the other. She said that she just could not make that important decision in such a short time. I bade her goodbye and left the next morning with a broken heart. I stayed with a preacher of one of the churches in Houston. He never said so but I am sure he wondered how such a mopey, introverted person could be an effective missionary. I am sure that my internal, crushed spirit manifested itself outwardly.

During these months I had found out that my overseeing congregation in Childress, Texas had decided to withdraw their oversight and the support they had been furnishing. Also during these same months Carl was speaking to churches in the Alabama, Tennessee area. He had met and married Frankie during that same time. His sponsoring congregation had been and still was the church in San Angelo, Texas. Carl had found out that I had lost my support and when he mentioned it to his overseeing elders they said they would take over my oversight and support. It was for this reason that I was scheduled to go from Houston to San Angelo to make final preparations for our return to Italy. I decided that on my way to San Angelo I would drop back by Garland. For those of you who do not know your Texas geography that's like going from Memphis to Dallas and dropping by Oklahoma City on the way. I arrived in Garland unannounced and went to the clinic where Doris worked. When I walked in her mouth dropped open, followed by the logical question, "What in the world are you doing back here?" I told her that I had made a little detour but wanted to see her again before going to San Angelo to make our return ship reservations. She, of course, was very surprised to see me but pleased. She told me that her family was going to a church picnic at the park that evening and that they were going with a family that lived a few houses from them. One member of that family was a young man she had known all her life and who was home on leave from the navy. She said that she knew he considered it a date with her. She said, however, that I should go to her sister and brother-in-law's where I could stay and come to the picnic with them. I did so and went with them to the park. There were quite a number of church people there and we played games, ate, etc. and all went well. At one point I told Doris that I would come by and pick her up after her friend had taken her home. We then went for a drive and a long talk. It was a very pleasant evening and among other things I told her that it was probably for the best that she decided not to marry and come with me to Italy because I had observed how attached she was to her close-knit family. I then added that she could probably not adjust to a different culture so far from home. She did not show it but I found out later that the reverse psychology worked. My words cut to the quick and she thought, "How dare him question my resilience and ability to adjust."

Anyway, I took her home and we said our last goodbye. When I arrived at San Angelo I found Carl and his new bride, Frankie. The congregation there was sponsoring and supporting both Carl and me. Carl had made his speaking tour in some states east of Texas and Oklahoma. He met Frankie very quickly after he arrived and the love bug bit immediately. They, in fact, were already married at this time. That is the reason Frankie was there with him. We all stayed with the preacher there and in fact, I can still remember his name, Harrison Mathews, a wonderful preacher and Christian man. The next morning we headed together with him and one of the elders to the travel agency to make our ship reservations for our return to Italy. On the way Harrison decided to stop by the church building. When he came out he handed me a letter. Guess who? It was from Doris and she said that she had decided to take the leap. What a joyful morning that was. In talking to the travel agent he told us that there were no tickets left on ships for Italy for the next few months. The only thing available was first class on the Queen Elizabeth that could take us to France. The elder said "you've got to get back to your work,

ON TRIAL IN ITALY for Preaching the Bible

let's do it". Reservations were made on that ship for the four of us. The departure date was six weeks later.

That, of course, meant that we had a lot to do in a short time: make all the necessary plans for a traditional wedding and reception, decide what all Doris needed to take, buy the necessary suitcases and a trunk and get it all packed. The departure date of the ship from New York was July 1. The wedding was planned for and performed on June 18, 1953. For a honeymoon we went to a motel in north Dallas for two days. We wandered around downtown Dallas and went to a couple of movies. Then we went back to her parent's home to make final preparations for departure.

Howard Bybee

Carl and Frankie came by Sunday evening to drive us to New York. They had an old 1937 Ford that was not in very good condition. In fact, we knew that we would have to drive at night and sleep in the daytime because the motor would boil over if driven during the heat of the day. We made the trip in three days; I guess I had better say "three nights". We took our trunks and luggage to the docking area, found a used car dealer and sold their car. We spent the night at the Manhattan church of Christ, which at that time had some living quarters for missionaries passing through.

ON TRIAL IN ITALY for Preaching the Bible

TWO MISSIONARIES WITH NEW WIVES BACK TO ITALY

Finally the big day arrived. We boarded the Queen Elizabeth, the queen of transatlantic crossings back then. We were given very nice cabins as you can imagine, being first class. Our room servant told us when the meals would be served and also said that we could either go to the dining room or ask that the food be brought to our room. We normally ventured to the dining room even though our attire did not measure up to the other people who were real first class passengers. The stares didn't bother us when they brought the filet mignon and fancy sea food platters. We knew that very high class people usually traveled first class but were surprised to see someone as well known as Walt Disney. It was a very enjoyable trip. They had an excellent program for children, movies, and all the amenities you would expect on such a ship. We knew that the apostle Paul traveled quite a bit by ship while doing his mission work but doubted that his was quite as comfortable. The six days it took us to get to Cherbourg, France went by quickly. When we docked we collected our luggage and had the trunk and the large suitcases sent by train on to Italy. We took the train to Paris.

In order to make the picture clear I will have to backtrack a bit and tell you that before Carl and I went back to the U.S. for our speaking tours we drove our cars to Paris, stored them there then flew back to the States. During the time that we had been in Italy we had each purchased a very small Renault. They were made much like the VW Beatle but even smaller. They were also very inexpensive because we being

Americans but living in Italy did not have to pay any tax. When we arrived in Paris we went to where the cars were stored, loaded up and headed for Italy. Doris and Frankie enjoyed the drive because everything was new to them. They were particularly awed by the beauty of Switzerland which, of course, we had to cross. There were two things that stood out for them, the Alps and the Tobleroni. The Alps you know but perhaps not the delicious Swiss chocolate bars called Tobleroni. They could not get enough of this chocolate until the curvy mountainous roads began to take its toll and they both became very car sick. Anyway we made it on to Italy and to the home of Mel and Emily Pownall who lived in Como, just across the Swiss border into Italy. The Pownalls had done mission work in Milano and had just moved to Como.

We then decided the girls would stay with Mel and Emily while Carl and I went on to Florence to find a place for us to live. No mission work had been done in Florence and Carl and Frankie along with the elders of their supporting congregation decided that with the Lord's help they would start a congregation there. These elders in San Angelo who were also supporting Doris and me asked us to stay and help Carl and Frankie in Florence for three months before going to Padova where I already had a work started. Doris and Frankie stayed in Como while Carl and I went to Florence to find us a place for us to live. On our way Carl and I were talking about how difficult it would be on these two new brides who would suddenly find themselves having to adjust to a new marriage and a new and very different culture. We decided that we would pull a psychological prank on them which might help break the ice. We knew that apartment living in Italy in 1953, shortly after the devastating World War II which they had lost, was not so easy. First we searched and found a fairly private four room apartment with kitchen and bath. Then on our way back we devised a story we would tell Doris and Frankie. We

ON TRIAL IN ITALY for Preaching the Bible

told them that almost nothing was available but that we did find a family that would rent us two bedrooms and we would share their kitchen and bath with us. When we returned to Como and the girls heard this news their countenance dropped and they were stunned. We bade the Pownalls goodbye and drove to Florence. When Doris and Frankie saw the apartment we had rented they were overjoyed. They didn't speak to Carl or me for a couple of days but were in a very good mood.

Carl and I began reaching out in Florence for people who might be interested in studying the Bible. Since so many Italians were interested in learning English we began some free English classes. This gave us contact with people with whom we could develop a rapport then hopefully get them into a Bible study. It was a method that back then worked very well.

Soon the three months of our stay in Florence ended and we moved back to Padova. At least for me it was "back home to Padova" but, of course, for Doris it was all a new experience. We found a nice apartment just a couple of blocks behind the train station which had been completely destroyed during the war and had recently been rebuilt. We scrounged up enough furniture to furnish our apartment, at least with the necessities. It Italy when you rent an apartment you rent only the space. There is nothing built in, no cabinets in the kitchen, no closets in the bedroom, just the walls and floor. We did get set up comfortably enough. We soon found though that to keep a four room apartment warm was more costly than we had anticipated. We, therefore, moved our bed from the bedroom into the combined dining room kitchen so we could close off the heat in the two bedrooms and save money. Once Cline Paden, whom you will remember me mentioning, came to spend a couple of days with us. He, naturally, had to sleep in the unheated bedroom. The next morning he came into the dining room carrying a container of water that was in that room and it was frozen solid. It does get cold in that part of Italy during the winter.

The first Sunday we were there we met with the church that I had started two years earlier. There were eighteen members at that time. While I had been gone Rafaello, the ex-Catholic priest that I baptized in the Po River had done the preaching. The members were very glad that I was back and warmly welcomed my new bride, Doris.

At first they could not communicate much because of the language barrier. Two or three of them knew a smattering of English so they could talk a little. Even though having only Italian speaking people for friends is a very frustrating way to adjust to a new culture it is the best way to learn another language. Doris began to pick up Italian quickly and soon became close to some of the ladies in the church. One of my reasons for going to the States was to raise money to buy a church building. During my first two years there it had become obvious how difficult it was to keep a suitable meeting place rented because of the strong Catholic opposition to our work. More than once the local priest had convinced the owner of our meeting place to ignore his contract and force us to leave. Also a stable meeting place would give more credence to our efforts to build the Lord's church. I had been able to raise $20,000 during my speaking tour back home. The search for a place to buy occupied a great deal of my time during those first months. This, of course, made it more difficult for Doris to adjust to a new country and a new language but she did fine. I found a place for sale in the center of the city where they were remodeling from war damage and selling a part of a building and part of a courtyard. I was able to buy it for $12,000 and for the remaining $8,000 rebuild what we needed. It turned out to be a very nice and adequate meeting place and a great location. The church in Padova is still meeting there. It was much easier now that we had our own building and the church continued to grow. Opposition from the Catholic hierarchy, however, continued to manifest itself. One example concerns a Gospel meeting we planned.

ON TRIAL IN ITALY for Preaching the Bible

THE FIRST PUBLIC MEETING IN PADOVA

This brings me back to my story about the early years of the church in Padova. After things were going pretty good with the work we decided to organize a public meeting. We thought we would set our sights pretty high and ask for the use of a large civic auditorium in the center of town. In fact, for use of this facility application had to be made through the office of the mayor. I knew that my name on the application as an American non-Catholic missionary would send up red flags and get nowhere. Since Raffaello was Italian and a citizen of Padova we decided to make the application in his name. Lo and behold, it was approved. We therefore began advertizing by having wall posters put up all over the city. The posters gave the titles of the lectures for each night of the week. We knew that the people had never had an opportunity to learn what the Bible says about the major Catholic doctrines. Therefore the topics were along those lines, like, for example: Was Peter the first Pope? Does one have to confess to a Priest to be forgiven? Christ is our only mediator, etc. The posters also explained that the lectures would be presented by a Biblical scholar, Professor Fausto Salvoni and there would be open discussion after each lecture. About three days after the posters came out and one day before the meeting I received a special delivery note from the mayor. The note said that because they were going to have to do some repair on the meeting hall and the meeting would have to be cancelled.

During those years there was an American consulate in Venice, about twenty miles away. I went to the consulate's office and asked to speak to him. He received me and I told him that I was an American living in Padova and that I was being defrauded by the city officials. I told him about the plans for the meeting, the approval letter and the advertising we had done. I told him that we had spent a great deal of time and money on the advertising all of which we would lose if we cancelled the meeting at that late date. He first said that since this was a religious matter he really could not intervene. I responded that legally it does not matter what the subject matter is if fraud has been committed. I added that his job as an American consulate was to act in behalf of American citizens having problems in that nation. He finally said, "Well, what would you like me to do?" I said that all I was asking was that he contact the mayor of Padova and ask an explanation for the withdrawal of their approval of this request and proof of why they did not know about the need for renovations when they approved our request. He finally said that he would contact the mayor. He then instructed his secretary and interpreter to call the mayor and ask for an explanation. It turns out that his Italian secretary was an atheist and a member of the Communist party that was strong in Italy at that time. He, of course, was contrary to the Catholic domination and came down pretty hard on the Mayor who then quickly communicated to us that we could go ahead with the meeting. The hall was filled to capacity, about five hundred people, each evening and brother Salvoni did a marvelous job with his lectures.

During the next three years the church in Padova grew to more than fifty members. Brother Raffaello continued to do a great deal of preaching and teaching. We also trained some of the men of the congregation to teach some Bible classes and take turns in the preaching. Doris picked up the language quickly and endeared herself to the members of the church. A very special event helped in this process and that was the birth of Jennifer.

ON TRIAL IN ITALY for Preaching the Bible

During her pregnancy Doris got a taste of what Italian health care was like. Remember that this took place in 1954, still close to the end of the war. We did find a pediatrician and he saw her once during the nine months pregnancy. When I took her to the hospital for the birth he was not there and she was assisted in delivery by a midwife. Jennifer livened Doris' life considerably and was the attention getter at church. A newborn baby is always a joy and for the Italians her red hair made her exceptional. Doris also learned to adjust to some other unusual circumstances. There was a period when we had no car and had to get by with an Italian Vespa, motor scooter. It was exciting, with the three of us riding on the scooter, with Doris holding Jennifer in her arms.

ON TRIAL IN ITALY for Preaching the Bible

POLICE DISRUPT CHURCH SERVICE IN LEGHORN

During this period the church experienced more persecution. Lido Petrini, who had been a Catholic monk but had left Catholicism, contacted Carl Mitchell and told him he wanted to study the Bible. He soon became a Christian and, in fact, began to preach the gospel. Then not long after that it was decided that a congregation should be started in Livorno (Leghorn in English). It is fifty miles from Florence and only about seven miles from Pisa. We planned to begin a work there by holding a series of lectures. We found and rented an auditorium and advertised the meeting throughout the town. We selected Lido Perini to do the preaching for that meeting. We went to Livorno for the first night of that meeting. There was a good turnout for the meeting, probably sixty or seventy people. Lido took the pulpit and started preaching. Then about five minutes later Italian policemen came in, disrupted the meeting, arrested Lido and took him to the local jail. As soon as the police left with Lido I took the pulpit and began to preach about the Lord's church as it is described in the Bible and our desire to plant one in that city. As soon as the service ended I and three other missionaries went to the police headquarters where they had Lido incarcerated. We told police chief that they had no right to keep Lido in jail. He said that he was just doing his duty. We then told him that if he did not release Lido we would all voluntarily incarcerate ourselves and notify the media. The chief then told us that he would release Lido. But before we left the station some newspaper reporters showed up and said they wanted to talk with us, that they had already heard about the police disrupting our meeting and arresting Lido. Three of us missionaries agreed to meet with the reporters. We had a good conversation with them. They asked us details about our meeting and what had happened and also about what we teach. Some articles did then appear in the local papers and gave the church more free publicity.

THE CHURCH'S LAWYER AND ME EXITING THE POLICE

ON TRIAL IN ITALY for Preaching the Bible

**ME AND TWO MISSIONARIES
BEING INTERVIEWED BY REPORTERS**

Now back to our concluding days with the work in Padova. We decided at that point that it would probably be good to leave the church there on its own for a while in order that they might more quickly learn to accept all their responsibilities by doing rather than just by listening. We therefore made plans to return to the U.S. and booked passage on a transatlantic ship. This was the year 1956.

ON TRIAL IN ITALY for Preaching the Bible

BACK TO THE STATES FOR A WHILE

We went back and lived for a while with Doris' parents in Garland, Texas. I began looking around for a church that needed a preacher. We soon located with the church in Whitesboro, about eighty miles north of Garland. This was a rather small town and small congregation. It was during that time that Kevin was born. Doris did have to go to the neighboring town of Gainesville to a hospital for the birth. However, it was paradise compared to the conditions where Jennifer was born in Italy.

Life there was good and rather uneventful except for a trip to Washington D.C. that I will tell you about. The mission work in Italy continued to suffer persecution from the Italian police and government. They were still denying visas for our missionaries. Some were forced to return to the States because the Italian government would not renew their visas. Others had to go out of Italy into Austria or Switzerland every six months in order to get temporary visas. This was a long drive and very disruptive to the work. In 1956, while we lived in Whitesboro, five of the missionaries who had been involved in the mission work in Italy decided to go to Washington D.C. and try to get some help on this matter from our Senators and Congressmen. We each contacted the Senators from the state we were from. In fact, I contacted them from both Oklahoma and Oregon since I had lived in both states. We were very well received and able to set up several meetings with congressmen. Lynden Johnson who was then a senator from Texas was one who met with us. Christian Herter, who was then Secretary of State, met with us as well and he brought to the meeting some information concerning a treaty of reciprocity between Italy and the U.S. that was signed after the war. It was called The Paris Peace Treaty and one of the clauses in the treaty is as follows:

> *"The olitical clauses stipulated that the signatory should take all measures necessary to secure to all persons under (its) jurisdiction, without distinction as to race, sex, language or religion, the enjoyment of human rights and of the fundamental freedoms, including freedom of expression, of press and publication, of religious worship, of political opinion and of public meeting."*

Mister Herter pointed out to the Senators and Representa-tives present, that many Catholic priests receive visas and come to the U.S and are never denied for religious reasons and that the actions being taken against the missionaries of the church of Christ is contrary to the concept of freedom of religion. Following is a letter I received from Lyndon Johnson, who was a senator at that time, regarding the matter:

Within a few weeks of this meeting our mission - aries began to receive their visas. In fact, after that all non-Catholic religious groups working in Italy began to experience much more freedom.

ON TRIAL IN ITALY for Preaching the Bible

OUR RETURN TO ITALY IN 1958

After a couple of years we felt the Spirit calling us back to Italy. While in Padova I had made some contacts for Bible studies in the city of Vicenza, the closest neighboring town to Padova with about 150,000 population. I had thought for some time that starting a church in Vicenza would be a good way to expand the Lord's work in Italy and that it would also be an encouragement to the church in Padova. After thought and prayer we decided that we would do just that if we could find a church to support us. We began spreading the word about our plans and were blessed that the Austin St. church in Garland agreed to take our oversight and furnish our support. We again sold our furniture, packed up and headed for New York to catch the ship. This time we traveled to New York by train. We boarded the ship and sailed across the Atlantic, through the Strait of Gibraltar into the Mediterranean Sea and on to Genoa, Italy. It was nothing like the Queen Elizabeth we sailed on the first time. The difference was like that of a Model T Ford compared to a Mercedes. It was, however, adequate and even third class was not all that bad. That journey took us thirteen days. We enjoyed the trip except when we would hit a storm. Even our children got seasick and Jennifer, now four years old, kept lying in the bunk saying, "No, no want it."

We docked in Genova. Bernard and Joan Howell, missionaries who had worked with us briefly in Padova picked us up and took us to Vicenza. At that time there was an American military base in Vicenza. We found out, in fact, that there was a church of Christ group meeting on the base. We found an apartment, bought furniture and got settled. We attended services with the military group and explained to them our plans. This turned out to be a blessing because some of those members offered to help any way they could. Our first priority was to find a place to meet in downtown Vicenza. We found a vacant store building not far from the center and rented it. It was in very poor shape esthetically and needed a lot of cleaning and painting. Several of the American brethren pitched in and really helped. I must mention in particular, the Ed "Benny" and Frances Mitchell family. They helped us many times and in many ways. (I will make an unusual entry at this point to mention that their son Paul, who was a preteen in those days, has kept in touch with us through the fifty-five years since that time. He is a member of the church in East Tacoma, Washington. Paul writes, finds, and distributes excellent articles and material concerning the faith. You might find it interesting and stimulating. He can be contacted at: PaulMitchl@aol.com)

Once we got the meeting place in order we planned and advertized a series of lectures and brother Fausto Salvoni agreed to hold the meeting for us as he had done in Padova. We did the wall posters again because that was still the standard way of advertizing public events. The meeting was well attended. In fact, our meeting place that would hold about seventy people was full each night. It was our custom back then to have an open question and answer period after the lecture. There were two or three men in the audience who tried to contradict what brother Salvoni had taught. We found out that they were Catholic priests disguised as normal citizens. At that time Catholic priests always wore robes, these men did not. The characteristic way Fausto handled opposition was very interesting. He would restate the opposing view, improve on it then show by the Scripture how it was erroneous. We announced each night that beginning the next Sunday morning we would have a worship service in accord with Biblical teaching. About twenty-five people came on Sunday and continued to come. Some were willing to do private Bible studies and within a short time some confessed Christ and were baptized. We at this time had another interesting but typical incident. The owner of the building we had rented came to see us and said that we would have to leave because we had deceived him. When we asked he said that we did not tell him that this was going to be a church. We said, "Well, let's look at the contract." The contract stated that the property would be used for public meetings and that if he would like he could take it to court because it was obvious to us that the contract clearly described what the building would be used for. He left in a huff. We did not see him for several days then he came back but with a very different attitude. He was very kind and courteous and said that he was sorry and that he would tell us the truth. He said the local Catholic priest came to his meat market and told him that if he did not get us out of his building he, the priest, would tell all the people in that part of town not to buy meat from him. This was in line with what the local Catholic authorities had been doing since we started our evangelistic work. In fact, Following is an article from a local Catholic bulletin called *"La Voce Dei Berici"* published April 29, 1959:

> *"In these days, numerous families of the city (we do not know if people outside of town have received such) have received cards from the so-called "church of Christ". By means of the cards the families are invited, not only to participate in the public meetings, but also to choose from other forms of 'study' which are: (a) Bible correspondence course, (b) Free tracts, (c) A private visit to individual homes to propagandize this same sect. We believe it opportune to again report the words that His Excellency Monsignor Bishop said to the faithful ones of the city last June when the first meeting of the American sect was organized. "Catholics are not permitted to participate in such meetings; He who participates would commit a grave sin against the Faith. In*

> fact, the law of God commands us not to unwisely expose our own faith to dangers. Furthermore, the law of God commands us not to make a scandal by participating in such similar manifestations which were promoted in this city with the evident purpose of planting error, degrading the Catholic religion, insulting the Virgin Mother of God, the saints and the Pope in Rome. Moreover, the Catholics that participate in such acts of worship of this sect would be in danger of excommunication. Also those who accept any of the other forms of propaganda mentioned above would commit as serious a sin as if he actually attended the public meetings."

It is no wonder the man who had rented his store to us said, "I will be ruined by the priest's announcement if you do not leave my building." We told him that since he was honest about it we would look around and if we found another place we would move. We did, in fact, soon find a much better place. It was on the ground floor of a new very tall apartment building located on the major thoroughfare leading through Vicenza.

During that time the church continued to grow. All age groups of people were converted. I worked particularly hard with the young men who had been converted, encouraging them to begin doing some teaching and preaching. My hope was that they would develop into capable leaders of the congregation. In some cases I let them perform the baptisms of new coverts. While in that location the church grew to about thirty-five members. During this period we had a very interesting visitor, a famous American singer. Many of you will remember the years that Pat Boone became one of the best male vocalists in the U.S. with several hits on the charts. One day I got a phone call and it was Pat Boone who was with a large filming crew in Venice. He had come to make some films for Television. He was a member of the church of Christ and asked me about coming to Vicenza the following Sunday to join us in our worship service. Naturally I told him they would be very welcome. On Sunday morning he and his wife Shirley came. A number of the Italian Christians knew about Pat and his singing career and were very excited that they had come. After services Pat and Shirley went with us to our home for a brief visit then returned to Venice. The next day there was an article in the Italian newspaper that said basically: "Pat Boone, who is in Venice making films, visited Vicenza yesterday and enjoyed seeing the sights of our city." That is an example of how the journalists, all the city officials and everyone with influence bowed to the pressure of the local Bishop and tried to ignore our work and even our existence.

ON TRIAL IN ITALY for Preaching the Bible

A NEW SON AND A SUMMONS TO BE PUT ON TRIAL

At about that time Doris and I had heard that several of the missionary families had begun adopting orphaned children. One family got in contact with an adoption agency in Germany and was told that there were still many children there that needed adoptive families. Quite a number of them were fathered by American military personnel during and after the war. Since we were considering another child we decided to look into it. We were soon told of a young lady who was about to deliver and wanted to give the child up for adoption because there was no way she could support it. We worked out all the details and made plans to go to Germany to get him. I made plans for one of the young Italian Christians to preach the Sunday we would be gone. We drove to Erlangen, Germany and in a few days were able to return with our precious Kyle who was six weeks old.

When we arrived back home in Vicenza on a Sunday evening I found an interesting item in our mail. It was a court summons informing me that I was to be put on trial the following Wednesday. There were no more details in the summons except the name and address of a lawyer I was supposed to contact. I went to see him the next morning, a lawyer named Ettore Gallo. He brought out some papers and said that I had been accused of defamation of the state religion and distributing literature without a permit. I, of course, was interested in the details and he showed me a paper the justice system had given him. The paper was a sermon outline on the topic of "The Worship of Relics and Images". I realized quickly that this was the outline of the sermon that had been preached the Sunday I was gone by one of the first Italians to be baptized the year before, Silvio Caddeo. He was a very zealous and intelligent young man.

The sermon outline had been distributed at the church service as were all of our sermons and Bible lessons. Mr. Gallo also explained that he had been made my court appointed lawyer and that I had the option of using his services or finding another lawyer. I thanked him and told him that I would let him know. I did some investigating and found out that Mr. Gallo was considered one of the best lawyers in the city. I then told him that I would engage him in my defense. He said that the trial was scheduled for two days later, on Wednesday. The trial was set up in an unusual manner; in fact, the procedure was called in Italian *'direttissimo'*. That means the fastest most direct method possible for a trial to take place. He said that this procedure was normally used only in extreme cases such as terrorism, treason and things of that nature. He said that his first move would be to object to the procedure and insist on a normal trial where he would have time to prepare his case and I, as the defendant, would be interviewed by the prosecuting attorney as is always done.

We went to the hearing on Wednesday and Mr. Gallo prevailed in his approach and the trial was postponed and put in the category of more common trials. This normal procedure usually took two to three months. About a month later the prosecuting attorney called me in for an interview. The first thing he did was to bring out a copy of the sermon outline and ask me if I had done it. When I said "no" he almost dropped his teeth he was so surprised and confused because he and all the judicial officials had assumed that I had preached the sermon. However, I knew that the trial would proceed and that they would prosecute the Italian young man who had

ON TRIAL IN ITALY for Preaching the Bible

prepared and preached it. I did not want that to happen because of his being a new Christian and I knew that their courts would deal much more harshly with an Italian than with someone from another nation. Therefore, I told him that I would take responsibility for the sermon. He was very relieved and told me that I would be notified when the trial was to take place.

Finally the date was set about a month later. News about this trial had gone far and wide. The news media had picked up on it and it was in newspapers both Italian and American. In fact, Doris' parents in Garland, Texas knew about the trial before we did, even before we returned from Germany. The day before the trial all of the missionary families in Italy came to Vicenza. There were seven missionaries in Italy at that time so we had a house full. In fact, some of the couples slept in a building nearby that was under construction. The lawyer told me that during the trial I would have the opportunity to speak in my own defense. The courtroom was packed with people the day of the trial. All of the Christians from Vicenza and Padova came. There were also quite a few from the news media and many just curious. The trial was presided over by three judges who would pronounce the verdict. My lawyer made an excellent defense almost all on legal grounds pointing out that there was nothing in Italian law that would indicate that what I had been accused of was a crime. He pointed out that all the laws that gave the Catholic Church political power had been negated by Italy's loss of the war and the fall of Mussolini and Fascism. I was then given the opportunity to speak. I told them that I was very surprised to be on trial in a nation where the predominant religion taught that the Bible is the word of God, and the only thing I had done was teach the Bible. We had noticed that it was not readily available to the people and people were not encouraged to read it. In fact in years past the Catholic Church had forbidden the reading of the Bible by the common people. I said that I doubted that the even three judges presiding here at the trial had ever read the New Testament. I went on to explain that the sermon, the outline of which was the basis of my trial was simply a Biblical study on the subject of the worship of images and relics. I said that it would be evident from even a casual look at the outline that it was mostly quotations from the Bible. I went on to explain that our goal is simply to return to the Christianity described in the New Testament as it existed in the first century. I spoke for about fifteen minutes to a very quiet audience. When the prosecuting attorney took the stand he said that he had never tried a case like this one before and that truthfully he did not believe a crime had been committed. That ended the trial and the judges took only about five minutes to give a verdict of "not guilty". Once again the Lord had provided a helping hand and a way for the church and our efforts to become better known.

As we continued our work it became evident that the trial produced other blessings. We never saw the police parading in front of our meeting place again. Neither was the plainclothes policeman present at our meetings. Before the meeting there was almost always a disguised policeman present at our services and, of course, he was the one that had taken the sermon outline to the police station. It was also obvious that the Bishop of the city had advised the chief of police to try to find some way to get rid of us. In fact, one day I asked Mr. Gallo, my lawyer, why a man of his reputation would be appointed as a court attorney. He said that he had talked to some of the court officials and they told him they were very uneasy about this case and afraid of international repercussions that would reflect badly on the city of Vicenza. They said they knew it was motivated by the religious authorities and they decided it would be best to appoint a competent attorney, so they chose him. It was nice to feel free of oppression and the number of members continued to grow. We began to talk about our need for a permanent meeting place where the church of Christ could become a more stable fixture in the minds of the people of Vicenza. All of the members were part of the working class and had little or no savings. They all said that they would be willing to work and help remodel any structure if we could find one that could be made to fit our need. Doris and I decided that it would be wise for us to make about a three month trip to the States to raise money for a building. Our supporting elders at the Austin Street church in Garland, Texas agreed with that and said they would help in raising the funds.

ON TRIAL IN ITALY for Preaching the Bible

ANOTHER TRIP HOME ON A SHOESTRING

    We were always looking for ways to cut corners and I had found one in regard to transportation. Since we were American citizens living in Italy we found that we could go to the Volkswagen factory in Germany and get a Beetle at a very low price since we had to pay no taxes. I did that and used the car about a year before we planned this trip. We found that we could take it on the ship with us at a lower cost than for the family to travel by plane or train from New York to Dallas. We booked passage on the Leonardo da Vinci passenger liner and again crossed the Atlantic. An interesting thing happened to Jennifer on this trip. Some months prior to that trip she had started taking piano lessons. During the crossing the ship's activity director planned a talent show, as they were asking for volunteers we volunteered her to play a piece. She, of course, in that amount of time had not learned but a song or two. She, though, had learned the little song *"Per Elisa"* pretty well. Everybody applauded, especially Doris, Kevin, Kyle and me. When we arrived in New York and were able to retrieve our VW Bug, loaded it with all our things and headed for Texas. Naturally five people and all the luggage necessary for three months would not fit inside the little car so we also had a rack of luggage on top of it. Consequently that slowed us down considerably going up any incline but amazingly we made it all the way.

    It was a joyful reunion especially with Doris' mom and dad who had not seen their grandkids for three years and children change drastically at their ages: Jennifer seven, Kevin four and Kyle two. It was a new country and a new culture for our kids. As we drove into Garland they kept asking why people were selling their garages because they saw signs everywhere saying "garage sale". I spoke to a lot of churches and I did receive commitments for twenty thousand dollars. From the research I had done before we left Vicenza it seemed that that would be sufficient. The real highlight of the trip was obtaining Kyle's American citizenship.

During that visit home we did take a trip to California and, in fact, took two of Doris' nieces, Linda, now Jasper, and Cherry, now, Edwards. We, of course, showed them the highlights along the way: the Grand Canyon, the Painted Desert, etc. We went to my sister, Thelma's, in Manteca, CA. We also visited Carl and Frankie Mitchell, our missionary buddies, who were then living in Los Angeles. While there we also went to Disneyland. It was lots of fun and we did have somewhat of a trying event. We were walking everywhere with the kids in tow. At one point Doris told me to keep an eye on Kevin and she would watch Kyle. As usual I was a little overconfident and thought it would be a simple task. Shortly thereafter Doris said: "Where is Kevin?" I looked around and, behold, he was nowhere to be seen. Doris, of course, panicked and I felt very uneasy myself. We decided to look for a few minutes before going to the people in charge. In fact, in just a few minutes here he came holding a man's hand. Doris ran and grabbed him, naturally shedding tears. The man with a smile said: "I guess this is your child." We thanked him and that was about the end of a very pleasant day. Another interesting thing happened while we were still in L.A. Linda and Cherry, who were teenagers at the time, had a crush on Pat Boone, as teenagers do with celebrities. Since they knew that we were acquainted with Pat and Shirley they wanted us to give them a call. We did and, in fact, Shirley invited us to come to their home and swim in their swimming pool. That was a very memorable day for those girls and, of course, we enjoyed it also.

ON TRIAL IN ITALY for Preaching the Bible

BACK TO ITALY AGAIN

We drove back to Garland and soon began making plans for our return to Italy. After visiting family and friends a few days we packed up and took a plane to New York. One of the rare times we went by air. We went to the ship docking area and met up with Joe Gibbs and family. Interestingly of the seven times we crossed the Atlantic it always turned out that another missionary family was on board with us. We had a nice leisurely ten day trip from New York through the Strait of Gibraltar into the Mediterranean then on to Genova which was always our docking and departing port. If I remember right there was only one seasick inducing storm during the trip. We then went on back to our home in Vicenza. An interesting linguistic phenomenon took place when we arrived. We had become very good friends with our next door neighbors and they had kids about the same age as ours. When we came up in front of our house to unload their kids ran out to greet us. They began talking and asking questions and our kids answered immediately but in English. Of course that is explained by the fact they had been speaking only English for the past three and a half months. It took them about half an hour to get minds back in gear and start speaking Italian.

The Italian Christians were all happy we were back and the church had done well. As had been my plan I began contacting real-estate agencies and looking for an adequate building we might buy and renovate for the church. We looked for some time and did not find anything that looked interesting. One day an agent came by and said that he had found a store for sale on the main street of town. We went to see it and it was in a perfect location and would require a great deal of work but had very good possibilities. We met the owner and found out that the asking price was about the exact amount of money I had raised. I made him an offer about two thousand less than he was asking and he accepted. We made an appointment to meet at a notary's office a few days later. The morning we were to meet to sign the papers the real-estate agent called and said that the owner decided not to sell his store. He did not give any details. We, of course, were very disappointed and started looking again. A month or so passed and we found nothing.

One day I had to go to the store to buy some shoestrings. It so happens that the shoe store was just across the street from the store that we had hoped to buy. After getting the strings I decided I would go in and ask the owner why he had decided not to sell. When I introduced myself and asked him his mouth dropped open and he said, "What do you mean? The agent told me that you had decided not to buy." I knew immediately that the Bishop or the local Catholic church had contacted the agent and demanded that he foil the transaction. The owner of the store also realized that that was the case. We then made another appointment with the notary and met there a few days later. As we were sitting in the waiting room visiting he said that this was an especially happy day for him. He then explained. He said that some years previously he owned a house and a few acres near a Catholic church on the outskirts of town. He said there was a property between him and the church building. At one point that property came up for sale. He really wanted it and immediately went to his neighbor and they made an agreement for him to buy it. He didn't think they needed to sign anything because they had been friends for years. Then a week or so later he found out that the priest of that church put pressure on his neighbor and convinced him to sell it to him instead of to the store owner. He said that he had been hoping for years to find a way to get back at the priest and today was the day.

We closed the deal and both left very happy. As I mentioned the building needed a lot of renovation work. In fact, a large room behind the entrance room is where we planned for the church to meet. However, the ceiling was not high enough. The men of the congregation came every evening after work for weeks; we took up the floor and dug down about two feet. An interesting thing happened while we're doing that. At one point we hit solid rock. We wondered, "What in the world?" We dug around it and discovered that it was an ancient capstone that once sat on the top of a column in either a cathedral or some public building hundreds of years ago. It was huge, weighing probably three hundred pounds or more. The Italian brethren explained to me that the city had an ordinance stipulating that if anything of antiquity was found and reported the work site would be confiscated and halted until the city workers could do more digging and investigating. They said that it would take months possibly even longer for us to get back in control of our building. In fact, one of the Christians helping us worked at the city hall. He and all the others said that we must not report it so we just dug a little deeper hole and it is still there. Finally the building was completed and we began holding services there. The baptistery was one we had carried from meeting place to meeting place while we were renting meeting places. It was a large chest we had built, just barely narrow enough to go through a door and long and deep enough to put a step down bottom in it and made the inside water proof. We installed that at the back of the auditorium where we had services. It was the site of many happy new births while we were there and, in fact, still is.

We had a good family life during that period. The kids were all in school and doing well. There were some differences from the American school system. Each student had to wear a uniform all of the same color, usually black, sometimes white. They were similar to a dress that came just above the knees. Things like that don't bother kids as long as everybody does it. The lower grades held class only to one o'clock but all of the schools went also on Saturday. One interesting thing of a religious nature happened to Jennifer when she started to school. In their subject matter they had also a class in religion, meaning, of course Catholic doctrine. They would have the kids participate in prayer, do the rosary, make the sign of the cross, etc. We thought that would not be a good thing for Jennifer to participate in so we talked to the teacher. We explained that Jennifer was not Catholic and would not be participating. The teacher took that to mean that we wanted her taken out of the class during that period. We found out some days later that she did send Jennifer out during that class and Jennifer, at her age, did not totally understand. She thought she was being punished because sending kids to sit in the hall was used as one of their forms of discipline. This was somewhat upsetting to her and when we found out we went back and talked to the teacher again. We explained that Jennifer would not participate in the religious activities but that we did not mind her remaining in the class room. We thought, in fact, that it could be a learning experience. We would discuss with her the things they were teaching and compare it to what the Bible says. It worked out fine. Her elementary school years were very satisfying. Interestingly, in the Italian elementary system a teacher starts out with a first grade and stays with the same class for five years. Fortunately Jennifer's teacher was not a religious bigot, as many were. She was a sweet lady and a good teacher so it worked out well for her. I will not go into detail about Kevin and Kyle's Italian schooling. Most of the differences have already been explained. They did fine during that time. Kyle was somewhat at a disadvantage because his male teacher was truly a religious bigot. He tried to push Catholic doctrine but Kyle ignored it and did okay. They made it through and got a good secular education.

I was very busy during those years with my church work and evangelism. I did a lot of personal work and worked hard at getting the members also involved. I did, though, try to spend as much time as I could with the kids. We would play together quite a bit in the back yard. At one point I began a building project. From one of our previous overseas trips I had several crates made of plywood. I decided to tear them apart and build a playhouse for the kids. It turned out pretty good for an amateur carpenter. Then one day we decided to make an overnight trip to the mountains. There is a range of mountains about twenty-five miles from Vicenza. Part of the planning for the adventure included putting the playhouse on top of our Opel station wagon. It was pretty tall but we did get it up there. After we took off we realized we needed gas and stopped by a filling station. However, as sometimes happens when I am trying to get everything together and my mind is cluttered I get a little distracted and it happened. I drove up to the gas pumps without noticing they had a cover above the pumps. Fortunately I was not going fast when the playhouse on top of the car hit the cover. It did make quite a noise and got everyone's attention. Thankfully it did not do any real damage to the cover and not a lot to the playhouse. I was able to repair it upon arrival. We got pretty high into the mountains and started looking for a good camping spot. We would see a little turn off road and go down it looking for a spot. We did that several times and finally located a really nice flat area. We unloaded the house and made the kids pallets in it for the night. We let down the tail gate of the station wagon and Doris and I were able to sleep there. Naturally we hiked a bit around the area and the kids enjoyed it all.

As I have often said "in God's providence" one thing often leads to another. This turned out to be one of those cases. As the church in Vicenza began to grow I began studying ways to help them grow spiritually, get more involved, and form a close-knit family. The churches in the Rome area had purchased some property near the coast and built a Christian camp. It was used for youth retreats and even families. These thoughts crossed my mind while we were in the mountains near Vicenza. I knew we had very little money and that a Christian camp would cost a considerable amount. I began to include this thought and idea in my prayers. As I mentioned before, we also had a congregation of Christians at the American military post on the outskirts of Vicenza. They had always been willing to help the Italian church any way they could. I knew that some of the military Christians were very respected and influential men. In my mind the light bulb came on. I had heard that the military post sometimes gave away used equipment that they did not need. I decided to approach some of those Christian men with the idea of their checking with the base commander about the possibility of the base giving some used tents and camping equipment for a church camp. Lo and

ON TRIAL IN ITALY for Preaching the Bible

behold it all came to fruition. The base gave us four large tents, many cots, folding tables and chairs and other odds and ends. I told the Italian congregation about this and they were thrilled. They were willing to pitch in and collaborate in every way possible. Shortly thereafter I took some of the men to the mountains and showed them the spot we had discovered on our overnight playhouse trip. It was a rather isolated spot about a quarter of a mile off the main mountain road down a small, rocky but passable road. One of the first questions one of the members asked was, "Where will we get water?" We began to search and about a hundred feet down a steep slope we found a spring. I immediately thought of Luigi, a man who had married a lady from Holland and who owned an auto parts and equipment store. He and his wife were friend of ours and had been coming to church for quite a while. I was sure that he would have water pumps and would be willing to help us install one. That worked out, it was not an easy task but it was accomplished. That summer we had a very pleasant and productive Christian camp with some Christians also coming from neighboring congregations. That camp continued to function every year until we left Vicenza in 1968.

    I want to relate another thing that happened during that period. One of the elders of the Garland church that supported us during the ten years we were in Vicenza was Jack Davis. Jack was the elder that was most closely and emotionally attached to us during our time there. He was an amazing man especially his dedication to the Lord and his memory. One of the things I learned soon after I got acquainted with him was that he did not have al telephone directory of any kind. He knew them all by memory. Once while we were in Vicenza Jack and his wife Dorothy came to visit us. Naturally the Italian congregation was anxious to hear a message from him on Sunday morning. I sat in the front with Jack so I could get up and translate his message into Italian. I knew that he had never studied Italian or any other foreign language. Just as he got up and I started to get up he motioned for me to stay seated. I thought, "What in the world is he going to do?" He started speaking in Italian and went on and on. He talked on for ten or twelve minutes in very good Italian. The Italian Christians were amazed and Doris and I really were. We found out later his secret. He had written out his message, sent it to Earl Edwards, an ex-Italian missionary, had him translate it into Italian and record it on a tape. Jack listened to that tape until he had memorized the whole thing. Would any of you reading this like to try something like that?

A little before we left Vicenza, Rob and Evelyn Thompkins came over with the intentions of learning Italian and getting some experience in order to replace us when we left. This time on our way home we crossed the Atlantic by air. In fact, we made a stopover in England and spent a week with a preacher friend and his wife, Jack and Ann Exum who were doing mission work in Ireland.

The second thing I want to say about Jack has to do with our new adventure after we returned to Garland. During the years that I had done mission work I had often thought about the blessing it would be to our effort to spread the saving message if we could somehow get young people of the church involved with us. I knew that this experience, even for a limited period of time, would strengthen their faith and make them more productive Christians. Interestingly, Jack shared the same dream. Once as I was driving around with the family while in Vicenza I was talking about this idea and Jennifer who was then in the tenth grade in an Italian school spoke up and said, "If you get a program like that started I want to be a part of it." Then in 1969 we left Vicenza and sailed back to the U.S. Naturally, all our family and friends in Garland were glad to see us arrive.

A TWO YEAR MISSION PROGRAM FOR HIGH SCHOOL GRADUATES

We rented a house and purchased the necessary things to set up housekeeping. Before long I met with the elders of Eighth and Austin church and I began to tell them about my dream. Of course, Jack pitched in and helped me a great deal. After a bit they agreed that they would continue our support and I could begin recruiting young Christians for the two year mission challenge. I began speaking to congregations and youth meetings around the Dallas area. I simply explained the program and told the high school age Christians to consider giving their first two years after graduating to mission work in Italy. They would then either go to college or enter their career. I told them that I would give them Italian and Bible lessons as soon as they enrolled in the program. Rather quickly a number began to sign up. They would come to Garland one evening a week for training.

Austin Street Church of Christ sponsors second mission group

Howard Bybee

One thing we did at our first meeting was discuss a name for the program. There were several suggestions but the one that won the majority vote was "*Avanti Italia*" which in Italian means "Forward Italy". I then began organizing weekend retreats for the teams. These were held at various youth facilities around the Dallas area and served for more training. The young people really enjoyed it. We played games as well as study and train. I added another feature to the program just as a precaution. The plan was that when a team was formed and they graduated from high school they would be sent as a group, possibly two groups depending on how many were ready to go. They would go to work with an Italian congregation. They would either live with an Italian Christian family or two or three of them would share an apartment. Most congregations had either an American missionary or an Italian evangelist who would work with them. The team would be under the oversight of that person. Since these team members were relatively young, most of them eighteen.

One thing I thought about was that many parents might be a little afraid and concerned since their sons and daughters would not have any adult American supervision. So, another brainstorm, I decided to see if I could recruit a widowed Christian lady to go with each team. That was not really that hard to do. We found rather quickly the ones we needed. Finally in 1970 the first team graduated from high school and left for Italy. This first group went to work with the church in Vicenza. They stayed in the homes of Italian Christian families and spent their time becoming fluent in the Italian language and evangelizing. It rather quickly became obvious that the *Avanti* workers were chaperoning the chaperones. Of course, the chaperones were generally quite elderly and we know that younger people can much more easily and quickly learn another language. The team kept in close touch with the chaperone, translating for them and purchasing for them things they might need. The process that I just described was repeated for the next four years. Each year the team would go to a different city and work with the congregation there. It was rather amazing how well these young Christians adjusted to a foreign culture, learned the language, and did good work even though they were so very young.

As I mentioned earlier, while we were living and working in Vicenza and had just begun talking about starting a two year mission program for Christian young people Jennifer, who was then only in Middle School, said she wanted to take part in a program like that as soon as she graduated from high school. Well, the Lord does help us fulfill our dreams when they point in the right direction. She and her cousin, Terry LeFan, became part of one of the first teams. Their team went to help one of our missionaries, Joe and Jean Gibbs who were working to start and build up a congregation in Genova.

An interesting little unusual thing happened during this time. One Sunday afternoon our phone rang and I answered it shortly before I had to depart for a speaking engagement with a congregation in Dallas. The operator said, "This is a telegram and I will read it to you." She did and said, "I am eloping with or living with (I can't tell which it is) a Mormon". That was the end of the telegram. I was very disturbed and confused but since I was about to leave I decided not to tell Doris until after I returned from my appointment. As soon as I returned home I told Doris about it. She almost fainted and in a rather emphatic tone said: "Do you mean you got this information more than two hours ago and you have not done anything about it?" I said, "Yes" but added, "What could I have done?" We discussed it with some mental anguish and finally Doris suggested that since Jennifer and Terry did not have a telephone, we could call Joe and Jean Gibbs. I reminded her that at that moment it was about 3 AM in Italy. She said, "I don't care, we have to find out more about this now." So, we called and Jean answered the phone. Doris began immediately asking her if she knew anything about Jennifer. Jean recognized from her voice that Doris was very emotional and said: "Don't you guys realize what day this is?" From the other phone I spoke up and said: "This had better not be an April Fools' joke?" What I really felt in my heart was: "This had better be an April Fools' joke," and sure enough it was. To keep the record straight I must admit that through the years I had been quite a prankster and Jennifer was the brunt of several. She was getting even.

Jennifer and Terry did a good work in Genova. In fact, one of their conversions was a young lady from England who was, at the time, living in Genova. Her name was Phoebe Orr. She was an agnostic/atheist who lived with them for over a year. The *Avanti Italia* workers met the Children of God (a cult) and spent some time discussing with them. Phoebe hated them, but when we all left Genova she ended up joining them. It was very dangerous and scary for her. She tells some interesting stories about them. She knew that Dee Bodine, another one of the *Avanti* workers, had been moved to Mestre so she went there, found Dee and asked her to help get her out of that cult. The cult leaders tried to get her back but Dee and Janine kept her safe. She was baptized in their bathtub.

In working with the *Avanti Italia* program we were of course dealing with young people naturally some problems did arise. One interesting one was in regard to the regulations the Garland elders required the *Avanti* members to accept before they departed. One of the regulations stated that the members would not enter into any serious dating relationships during their two year mission. However, as we all know, the love bug cannot always be controlled. While working together one of the young men and one of the young ladies became enamored. In fact, it developed rather quickly and seriously, even to the point that they wanted to get married right away in the city where they were working in Italy. The elders reminded them of the regulations they had agreed to before they left for Italy and would not give their permission. However, the couple's feelings were so strong they decided they could not wait so they came home and got married. He, in fact, has been for many years an elder of a strong congregation in Tulsa. As I mentioned earlier, Elders in churches of Christ were not accustomed to overseeing a group of young Christians, especially in a foreign country. After four years of this program the Garland elders decided they did not want to continue overseeing it. That meant, of course that the program was being discontinued and I would need to look around for a church that needed a preacher.

ON TRIAL IN ITALY for Preaching the Bible

THE LORD POINTED US IN ANOTHER DIRECTION

I found out that a church in Bartlesville Oklahoma needed someone. I applied there and was accepted at the 6th and Dewey congregation that was located in the downtown area. By this time Jennifer was already in college. She went to Harding for a semester then transferred to Oklahoma Christian. Kevin was a senior in high school and Kyle a sophomore. Probably the most interesting things that happened during those school years for the kids were Kyle becoming a pilot and Jennifer finding a husband.

While she was at Oklahoma Christian Jennifer met Gary Williams. They began dating. One thing happened during that dating process that gave me the idea that we could get back at her for the Mormon trick she played on us. We learned that she had been reprimanded a few times by her dorm mother for coming in late. I knew well one of the Professors at O. C. I called him and ask him if he would cooperate with us on our trick. That is, he would send her a letter telling her that she had been suspended from school for three months for breaking the school's curfew rules. He did this and it gave her a shock, but after a bit she began to suspect something devious because the letter with the professor's letterhead had his name at the bottom but was not signed. He told us later that he just didn't have the heart to sign it.

The Bartlesville high school was one of the very few in the state that had a flight instruction class and single engine airplanes. Kyle took that class and learned to fly the plane to the point that he made a solo flight from Bartlesville to Lubbock, Texas and back. He made the trip fine with a diversion or two around storm clouds but decided that he had rather travel by land and that was the end of his aviation career. After four years with the church there the congregation decided to leave the downtown area and build a new building on the outskirts. At that point they also decided to begin in their new building with a new preacher. That, of course, necessitated our looking for another congregation that needed someone.

We found an ad in the Christian Chronicle saying that the church in Gruver, Texas was looking for a preacher. On the map we discovered that Gruver is located in the Texas panhandle about thirty miles south of the southern border of the Oklahoma panhandle. We decided to visit them and check out the situation. We knew that it was a small town but were a little surprised to learn that the town had only 1,025 inhabitants. We were pleased, though, to learn that it had a nice congregation for such a small place. They had a very nice building, two elders, and about 125 members. After our visit they expressed a desire for us to come and work with them. We decided to do that and made our move. As we were considering moving to another congregation we had one desire in mind that we wanted the elders to approve before concluding an agreement. That desire related to the love in our hearts for the congregations we had initiated in Italy. We thought it would be good for us to keep in close contact with those congregations and to visit them if possible every year. The Gruver elders agreed that we could take a three week vacation period each year to make that visit.

Our time with the Gruver church was a pleasant time in our lives. This was, of course, a farming community. Many of the members farmed very large plots of land with huge, sophisticated machinery. They raised mostly wheat and corn. One of the pleasant things about the corn fields was that many pheasant lived there. This offered the opportunity of occasionally participating in large group pheasant hunts. The group would line up each in his own row and walk down the field keeping abreast of each other and shooting the pheasant as they flew up, or at least trying. At that point in our lives I began to think a little more about the future than I had before. I had learned that church leaders for the most part were very prudent with their use of church funds. Consequently they usually spent as little as possible on things they needed which included what they paid their preacher. Since there were no guidelines usually the elders never included a retirement fund in the preacher's salary. Doris and I realized this and decided we might do something on our own that would help us down the line. We knew that the Philips Petroleum Company had one of their branches in Borger, a fairly good size city about forty-five miles south of Gruver. We learned at that time that this company was expanding and had purchased two city blocks in a residential area. Their plan was to sell those houses to people who would move them away. This meant, of course, that they would sell them for very little because of the cost of house moving. Doris and I decided to buy a vacant lot in Gruver, buy one of those houses and have it moved there. We had the foundation dug, put in all the rebar ourselves, even in the driveway area, then arranged for a company to bring and dump the concrete. We were going to spread it ourselves thinking the trucks would spread it somewhat in the driveway as they dumped it. To our chagrin they put it in one big pile. That, as you can imagine, was the hardest manual labor either one of us ever experienced. Anyway, after spreading and smoothing it we survived. We did hire a couple of carpenters to make some modifications to the house and finish the project. We then rented the house and made one small step toward an eventual retirement fund.

I mentioned earlier our desire to visit the churches in Italy and encourage them. Finances, of course, entered the picture regarding this plan. Already a number of times through the years of our service in the Kingdom we had seen the providence of God at work in our lives. In regard to this plan we saw God's hand again. A brother from Nashville had begun an inexpensive tour of Europe for Christians, using chartered airliners. During those years chartered planes were much less expensive than regular scheduled flights. This brother from Nashville contacted me and asked me if Doris and I would go as guides on one of his tours. We accepted, had a good tour, and got to visit with our dear brothers in Italy. I paid close attention to the organization and to the details during that tour: how to charter planes, how to rent busses, and make hotel reservations in Europe. By the time we arrived home I had already begun planning to organize, publicize, and lead my own European tours for Christians.

ON TRIAL IN ITALY for Preaching the Bible

A NEW DREAM REALIZED

Since leaving Italy I had continually prayed for my children in the faith there (an expression the apostle Paul used regarding those he led to the Lord). I had a great desire to pay an occasional visit to those Christians strengthen, encourage them and show them that they were near to my heart. I thought that taking tours would be a way to finance this dream. I then got busy making the arrangements for our tour. I say "our" because I knew that Doris would help and be a big part of it. I contacted some airlines about reserving a charter flight. I put together an itinerary with our first stop being London then Holland, Germany, Austria, Italy, Switzerland, and France. Our flight home would be from Paris.

I found a tourist agency that would contact good but inexpensive hotels for the various places we would stay overnight. I had already learned that the best place in Europe to charter tour buses was Belgium. There I found just what we needed. They agreed that the bus would pick us up at a port in Holland where the ferry from England docked and would take us to Amsterdam for our first night in Europe.

That worked well but the third year we did the tour we took two busloads, 90 people, and an exciting thing happened that I need to tell you about.

Everything went as usual and or first destination was London. We had a good visit there and naturally I had to hire two busses to take us to the coast to catch the ferry to Holland where we would meet the two Belgian busses. We left London and when we got to the harbor to catch the ferry we soon discovered that they had taken us to the wrong harbor. The harbor, where the ferry we needed was, was about forty miles up the coast. We took off for that harbor and the ferry we were supposed to catch had already left. They had ferries crossing the channel about every hour. We took the first one we could get, knowing that it would land in Holland almost two hours later than the time we had communicated to the bus company. You can imagine what fear and anxiety we had as we approached the harbor in Holland. As the saying goes, "The Lord helps even the incompetent." The bus drivers were there and they said they had expected us on the two previous ferries and were planning to leave after this one. We then went merrily on to Amsterdam stayed overnight, had a good visit there then headed for Cologne, Germany. It seems that that particular tour was somewhat jinxed as you can tell from what happened next. When we arrived about eight o'clock at the hotel where we had reserved rooms and dinner in Cologne the desk clerk said, "I am sorry but I have no reservations for your group." As I mentioned earlier I engaged a Tour company in London to make all the hotel reservations and, of course, I had sent them the money to do so. There we were ninety people expecting dinner and a bed. I was at my wits end and had no idea what we would do. Praise the Lord, one of the men in our group, Newman Bench, an elder at a congregation in Garland, TX, had a credit card. Back then, in 1979, that was a novelty. He graciously insisted that I use his card to get us rooms. Again, saved by the bell. However, the bus drivers had understood what was happening so they called their head office and found out that the bus reservation fund had not been paid either. I kept calling the tourist company in London and could not get them. The bus drivers said they were told to return to Belgium. By then it was midnight. I talked to the drivers and begged them to go on at least one more day. I guaranteed them that even if we did not get the money from the Tourist agency I would personally pay them. They agreed but said that's it

ON TRIAL IN ITALY for Preaching the Bible

unless the money comes through. The next day we were headed for Heidelberg. There we encountered the same thing, no reservations for dinner or the hotel. I paid for the dinner with Newman's credit card and also the hotel. *I must insert here that I did pay Newman back later.* However, Doris and I and a couple more stayed with Glen and Shirley Boyd, who were doing mission work there. The bus drivers were also ready to go back to Belgium but hey finally agreed to go on one more day. The next morning we loaded up and headed for Munich. On our way we passed near Stuttgart. I asked the driver to find and take us to the American Consulate there. When we arrived I took Newman with me and we asked to speak with the American Consul. He received us and we explained our situation. We explained to him that we were Americans who had been defrauded by a tourist agency in London. He said, "Well that's just a financial problem you have and I cannot get involved in matters of that nature." Newman spoke up and said, "Sir, I am a businessman and pay taxes, part of which goes to American consulates around the world that are there to help our citizens who are traveling in various countries and happen to encounter problems. I would strongly advise you to consider our plight and do what you can to help us. I would not want to contact any of our elected officials and report to them that you refused to give us any assistance." He immediately changed his attitude and asked, "What do you think I could do?" Newman told him that it would probably be very helpful if he would call our tourist agency in London and ask him why he had not paid our hotels thus leaving our tour group stranded. The consul immediately did just that. He fortunately got hold of the tourist agency manager, told him who he was and asked for an explanation. The manager said that he was sorry that he had placed the hotel payments in the mail a couple of days too late. He promised that the hotel in Munich and for the rest of the tour would be in order. We thanked the Consul and drove on. Thankfully, all was well in Munich and for the rest of the trip.

Almost all of our tours went well. We did, of course, always go by the cities of Padova and Vicenza, Italy where I had started churches. It was great to visit with my sons and daughters in Christ. Once we had an interesting side-trip when we visited Vicenza. About twenty miles from town was a relatively high flat-top mountain with a beautiful, interesting view. I decided we would drive up there for a picnic lunch. It was a very steep, rather small, curvy road. The bus driver had to back up and go forward several times to make some of the curves. We did make it to the top and spread out everything for our picnic lunch. As we were eating I explained to everyone that near the side of the mountain top was a ski lift that took people straight down the side of the mountain to a small village at the bottom. I asked people to raise their hands if they would like to take the lift down and the bus would pick them up there. The first person to raise their hand was the bus driver. Yes, we had lots of fun. We always visited Venice, Florence, and Rome before heading back to Paris for our flight home. The Rome traffic was always very intense. One year, though, it was what I with my Oklahoma background would call a 'doozy'. We were there the very day of the world soccer tournament was being held in Rome. If you are familiar with the popularity of soccer in Europe you will understand why we spent most of the day in the bus snarled in traffic because Italy had won the World Cup and everyone was in the streets either in cars or as pedestrians.

We finally did make it to our hotel about two hours later than we had planned. From there we made it back to Paris and on home. Well, that is probably enough about our yearly Christian tours while we lived in Gruver.

As, I am sure you have understood by now our hearts were geared toward mission work and the spread of the Lord's

ON TRIAL IN ITALY for Preaching the Bible

church in Italy and in Europe. By the year 1980 I had decided that I would like to go beyond preaching for a local congregation and concentrate on spreading the Lord's word in Europe. Being encouraged by a number of European missionaries I decided to leave local work and start a missionary recruitment program for the large un-evangelized cities of Europe. The Sycamore View congregation in Memphis, TN agreed to take our support and the sponsorship for this program. It was fine with their elders for us to live in Searcy, AR and make Harding University our base of outreach. Consequently we moved to Searcy to begin the new effort we were calling: EUROPEAN OUTREACH PROGRAM.

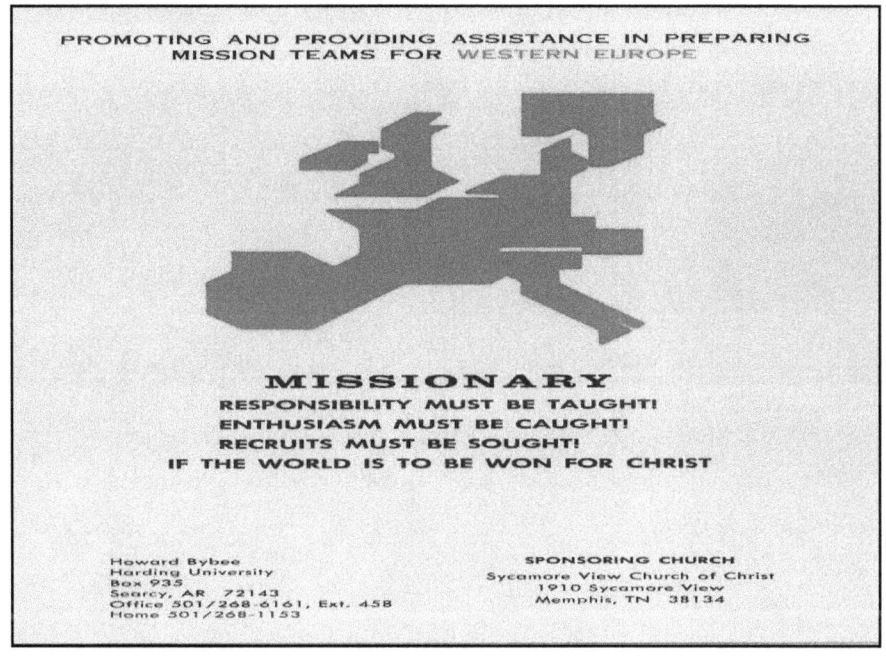

In the beginning of this work one of the European cities I concentrated on was Lisbon, Portugal. After a few months of work I succeeded in finding two couples that agreed to visit Lisbon and try to prepare a team to go there to establish the Lord's church. Interestingly one of these couples was Gary and Jennifer, my son-in-law and daughter. The other one was Scott and Gwen Bulmer. I went with them on the survey trip. It ended up that Gary and Jennifer were not able to move to Lisbon but Scott and Gwen did. They worked there for ten years and started a congregation.

BACK TO ITALY AGAIN

Then in 1980 the Southwest church in Jonesboro, Arkansas asked Doris and me if we would consider returning to Italy. This congregation some seventeen years previously had purchased the Bible School villa in Scandicci, on the outskirts of Florence and the elders served as overseers of that program. They started a Bible training program for young Italian college age Christian men and women. They selected two Italian missionaries, Earl Edwards and Don Shackelford, to direct the program and teach the classes. A number of American missionaries and Italian evangelists collaborated with and taught classes at the Bible School. In fact, during those years I took the train to Florence a couple of times and taught classes. Earl and Don consulted with the other missionaries in Italy about the direction the Bible School program would take. By that time all of the missionaries had learned from study, experience, and observation that there were many negative factors in mission work with the practice of putting native men who had learned to preach on salary from American congregations. This practice would cause those native preachers to depend on the American salary and consequently do very little to teach and encourage the Italian Christians to give generously in order to support their preacher. Because of this the director of the Bible School decided to make the program not necessarily a preacher training school but a program to give good Bible training to both young men and women. It was also decided that those who left home and moved to Florence could begin or continue their college training at the University of Florence and the Bible classes would be held in the afternoon and evening. This was especially appealing to young Christians in congregations scattered throughout Italy because since the end of WWII many cities had not reopened their universities. Therefore they were pleased to move to Florence both for the Bible training and the opportunity to take classes at the university. During the following years a good number of young men and young ladies attended and completed the two year schedule of Bible classes. They were therefore better prepared to help their congregations grow when they returned home. The return to the States of the Edwards and the Shackelfords and the closing of the Bible School program was a disappointment to the churches in Italy and to the elders of the Jonesboro congregation. They contacted Doris and me and told us they would support us if we would return to Florence and reopen the Bible School program. We accepted, once again sold our home, and boarded the plane for Florence.

During that period both Harding and Pepperdine Universities had been using the property for their Italian branch programs. Now that the Bible School program was reopening, both these universities purchased their own properties in Florence. As soon as Doris and I got settled I started visiting the congregations throughout Italy looking for young Christians that might be willing to move to Florence to take Bible courses. I found three young men and a young lady and started a series of Bible courses for them. Naturally we had to feed them so I began looking around the neighborhood for a cook. THIS TURNED INTO A LEGEND. We found Rosa, who lived nearby and worked from her home, not as a cook but as a seamstress, but she said she would take the job. I call it a legend because that was thirty-two years ago and she has satisfied the taste buds of everyone who has passed through the door of the Bible School and is still there cooking for the *Avanti Italia* workers. Rosa's husband, Felice, had retired from the Italian army. An interesting story developed from his military connection. As, I am sure you can imagine, a lot of olive oil is used in the Bible School kitchen. Felice brought several cases that had been given to him from the military deposit and stored them in our garage. To our chagrin, it was not very good olive oil, usually used only in cases of emergency. At that time the Bible School had an old and, I would add, practically worn out Volkswagen mini bus. In fact, the motor was so worn that it used a at least a quart of oil just to go to the train station and back, about an eight mile round trip. As was normal, we were strapped for money so I would take a can to the filling station down the street and they would give me oil that they had drained out of other cars. That worked pretty well even though a gallon would only make two or three trips to the train station and back. One evening rather late I had to take a couple of people to the station. I knew the car would need oil so I went into the garage and, sure enough, the light was burned out. I went by feel. I found a case and took a bottle. As I was pouring it into the motor it made a strange sound like it was more liquid than it should be. I stopped, turned on the headlights and looked at the bottle. It was wine. Fortunately I had poured only about three fourths of it into the car. I got some more of the old olive oil and topped it off. Would you believe, it made it to the station and back and didn't even hiccup.

ON TRIAL IN ITALY for Preaching the Bible

A NEW PROGRAM IS BORN OR I MIGHT SAY REVIVED AND UPGRADED

I continued to teach Bible courses to the three students who were there. I also spoke occasionally at the Harding group's chapel service. I thought this might be an opportunity to revive the *Avanti Italia* program and upgrade it from High School graduates to college graduates. I began to challenge these Harding students to commit the next two years after they graduate to spreading the Gospel in Italy. Two young ladies made that commitment. They were scheduled to graduate the next year, in 1986 and not only promised to return at that time but they did return. This was the beginning of the new college graduate *Avanti Italia* program. This gave a new direction to the use of the Bible School property. After the arrival of the first two Harding graduates to enter the new *Avanti* program the flow of new workers continued. Another Harding graduate, Jay Walls, followed those first two. I mention his name because he figures quite prominently in the ongoing development of the program. By the end of the first four years Doris and I realized that the program had great potential but if it was going to grow only if someone would visit our Christian colleges in the States and recruit new workers. Since Jay Walls was such a mature young man and a good worker we asked him if he would remain and direct the program for a while in order that Doris and I could return to the States to recruit. He agreed and again Doris and I crossed the Atlantic.

Howard Bybee

    We moved back to Searcy and I began visiting the various Christian colleges telling the students about an opportunity to spend the first two years after they graduate sharing the saving Gospel message with the people of Italy. I visited every Christian college in the church of Christ brotherhood and many campus ministries in state colleges. I invited those who were interested to come to Searcy for special weekend seminars with classes, discussion about the program and a ropes course to emphasize group activity and cooperation. During the next several years we sent new teams of five to seven workers every year.

ON TRIAL IN ITALY for Preaching the Bible

AN EXCITING DEVELOPMENT IN OUR SEARCH FOR A NEW DIRECTOR

By now you have understood that each director that agreed to move to Florence to direct the *AI* program agreed to stay anywhere from two to five years. At this point we were again at that crossroad. The current director had fulfilled his commitment and was returning home. I was still traveling looking for workers and now also looking for a new director. I went to the Dallas/Fort Worth area and this time Doris came with me. At that time Jennifer, our daughter, and Gary were living in Grapevine. Naturally while in that area we stayed with them. We were sitting in the living room just visiting and talking about our director search. At one point Jennifer looked at Gary and said, "Don't you think that you and I could move to Florence for five years and direct the program?" Gary looked somewhat stunned, was silent for a while then said, "Are you serious, we would have to give up our jobs, sell our home and furniture and where do you think we could find a church that would support us?" Jennifer calmly answered, "We could probably get our jobs back when we return or find new ones. As far as support is concerned we would tell the elders of the College church in Searcy, that had been giving some support to the *Avanti Italia* program, that we would do this only if they would provide our full support." After a bit more discussion Gary said, "Okay, let's give it a shot." Doris and I were somewhat stunned and amazed. We had a joyful prayer about it and decided that I would approach the elders with their proposal. I soon met with the elders, gave them copies of Gary's and Jennifer's resumes, and explained the situation to them. They were very impressed with their credentials and the fact that they would give up such good jobs and security to do the Lord's work for the next five years. They agreed to take their full support. That meant, of course, the die was cast. Gary and Jennifer, put their house on the market, sold their furniture, and made plans for their departure. They tell me that time lines are not that important in autobiographies but the event that I just described is a pretty important one in my life story. It took place the first five years of the 21st century. In other words, Gary and Jennifer moved to Florence in 2000 and directed the program for the next five years.

They guided those Christian college graduates in introducing their Italian students to the Bible and its message. Many Italians were and are anxious to learn English. Therefore the logical approach of the *Avanti* workers was to offer free English lessons using the Bible as the text. This was very effective and there was never a lack of Italians accepting this offer. The workers had the students read the Bible text in English

ON TRIAL IN ITALY for Preaching the Bible

and discussed it, making sure they understood. They not only gave lessons to their students but also made friends with them, inviting them to group activities, parties, refreshments, etc. They also invited them to weekly group Bible studies in Italian. Some of them attended regularly.

During this five year period while Jennifer and Gary were there Doris and I took every opportunity we could to go visit them. There were missionaries in most of the European countries. Every year a European lectureship was organized, each year in a different country and city. These lectureships gave Doris and me opportunities to go to Europe and, of course, we would also manage a trip to Florence for a good visit with our kids. One such lectureship that we attended was in Warsaw, Poland and another in Edinburgh, Scotland. Since Gary and Jennifer also attended these lectureships we did not always go to Florence before coming home. However, the year of the Edinburgh lectureship an interesting turn of events changed our plans a bit. We had gone to the lectureship with tickets a friend of Jennifer's had given us. They were what are called "space available" tickets that were very inexpensive. However, there were no reservations. You just go to the airport and if there are seats available on your flight you go. If there are no seats available on that flight you just wait for another flight and keep trying. We made it over with no difficulty. On our trip home we flew from Edinburgh to Dublin and had to change planes. As chance would have it there were no seats available and no other flights that day. It was going to be rather expensive for a hotel. We remembered that an airline called Ryan Air had cheap flights to many cities in Europe. We checked and sure enough they had a flight with a couple of seats to Florence. So, that meant more time with our kids, friends, and brethren in Florence. After a few days in Florence we started checking on space available flights back to the U.S. and were encouraged by the Alitalia agent to go to Milan and try. We took the train up there and with good results. That adventure was over. We managed to go to Florence every Christmas during the time Gary and Jennifer were there. Another milestone occurred during that time and that was my and Doris' fiftieth wedding anniversary. We, of course, wanted to share that special day with our kids so we made another trip to Florence. After we had arrived Jennifer told us that Rosa had invited us to her house for dinner that evening. When we arrived at her place we noticed a lot of people in her yard. As it turns out she had a long table set up in her front yard loaded with refreshments and the yard was filled with members of the church from Florence and other friends. There was also a big sign that read:

"HAPPY ANNIVERSARY"

We lived in Searcy during those years. My work was traveling, recruiting *Avanti Italia* workers, organizing, and directing the training program for the new recruits. Also, as the William's commitment was almost completed and their departure drew near I had to begin looking for a new director couple to replace them. I had become acquainted with David Woodroof who had worked in the media center at Harding for about ten years. During that time I also became acquainted with his father, Jim. He is a retired preacher and author of several books. He became interested in the *Avanti Italia* program and began helping me in recruiting, training, and fund raising. One day, during my continued search for a replacement for Gary and Jennifer David, told me that he was tired of the media center work he had been doing and would like to find something more challenging, in fact, he said that he and his wife Debbie had talked about applying for the *Avanti Italia* directorship. By that time I had uncovered two other couples who also expressed an interest. The *Avanti* committee met to consider the applicants and offered the position to David and Debbie. Thus in 2005 the Williams came home and the Woodroofs moved to Florence to guide and direct the *AI* teams. One of their responsibilities was also the maintenance and upkeep of the building that housed the program. We soon learned that in this regard we had made a good new director choice. The church had owned that building for fifty years and had not done much during that time to keep the property well maintained. David had done a lot of construction and carpentry type work. In fact, he had completely remodeled the house they had been living in. This experience and ability came in very handily. David did more maintenance, upkeep, and remodeling on the *Avanti* villa than anyone had ever done.

A 2,300 MILE TRIP THROUGH ITALY

As I mentioned earlier Jim, David's dad, had been helping me with the *Avanti* program. Jim also had written a book called, "BETWEEN A ROCK AND A HARD PLACE". This is a very good book especially for someone contemplating whether or not he could logically believe what the Gospels say about Jesus. The *Avanti* committee decided that this book would be very useful to the Christians and churches in Italy and they had it translated into Italian. Jim had told them that he would take it to Italy and distribute it to the congregations. He approached me and said, "You have to go with me because I must have someone who can interpret for me." So, off we go into the wild blue... well, let's just say that Jim and I went to Italy with the idea of visiting all of the churches throughout Italy. Jim would leave some books with each church, explain to them the basic message of the book and how to use it evangelistically. David had agreed to take us on this trip in his van. We headed south, visiting churches along the way. We went on to the island of Sicily, visiting the church in Catania and Palermo, which, if you know your geography, is all the way to the northwestern point of the island of Sicily. I had not been to Palermo for about fifty years. Doris and I had gone there shortly after the Don Shackelfords and Earl Edwards had gone there to start the church.

Again, as I said before, my autobiography mentor encouraged me to include as many humorous incidents as possible. Consequently I will recount something that happened on our first visit to Palermo. We stayed with the Don and Joyce Shackelfords. Charles and Carolyn Moore who were there at the time spent some time visiting with us. Chuck was a typical missionary, maybe a little more so in the prankster category. When he and Carolyn came over to the Shackelfords Earl had gone on an errand. Chuck explained to us that he had found at the hardware store putty that had the same color and consistency as chocolate fudge. So he had something interesting planned since he knew how much Earl liked fudge. After Earl came back and while we were in the living room visiting Chuck went into the kitchen and brought in a plate of chocolate fudge, at least that is what it looked like especially with a half pecan on top of each piece. I am sure that you, being an intuitive reader, have figured out what it really was. Yes, Earl came in, saw the beautiful plate of fudge and took a big bite. He immediately began to spit and sputter and we all had a good laugh. The story doesn't end there. Chuck laughed so loud and hard that his nose began to bleed. In fact, none of us were able to get it stopped and we had to take him to the hospital to have it packed. That is the end of the story except for the fact that Earl continued to say: "How sweet is revenge."

I guess that is enough about Palermo except to return to the story about my and Jim's visit to the church there. On Saturday evening, as planned, we met with the Palermo church, Even though it was a Saturday evening a large number of members came, and we gave them copies of Jim's book. They expressed their appreciation by having a snack of pizza and Sicilian pastries prepared in our honor. Then after our meeting and snack, about eleven o'clock, fifteen or twenty of them walked with Jim and me back to our hotel. The next day we headed back north. However, rather than backtrack through Sicily and Calabria we put our van on a ship and sailed to Naples. That finished the southern Italy part of our trip. As we headed north we, of course, soon came back to Florence. We stayed there only one night then left to visit the churches in the northern part of Italy. When we got back to Florence we had travelled about 2,500 miles. Jim and I then flew back home. We were thankful that the Lord had given us a good and profitable trip. In finishing this era of the *Avanti* program I will just say that David and Debbie stayed on directing the program until 2014. At that time a new couple took their place. This couple, Eric and Jessica Smith, are well prepared for this job because they had done the *Avanti* two year program a couple of years before, spending most of their two years in Taranto. This city is in the very southern part of Italy, actually located on the coast in the instep part of the Italian boot. In fact, this was the most challenging two year experience that any *Avanti* worker had ever done. The reason is that the farther south you go in Italy the more different and antiquated the culture becomes. However, they were able to do a very good work, strengthening the small congregation that had been started by an Italian evangelist. They had been back in the States for about two years and were pleased that the *Avanti Italia* committee asked them to replace the Woodroofs.

OUR CHILDREN'S CAREERS

I mentioned earlier about Jennifer and Gary going to Italy for five years to direct the *Avanti Italia* program. I want to say a word about her career and the interesting way it got started. After Jennifer had graduated from Oklahoma Christian, she married Gary Williams and they moved to Albuquerque, NM. Gary got a job as assistant minister at the Montgomery Blvd. church of Christ. By then they had two boys, Brock and Erik. Jennifer decided that she would not seek employment but stay home with the boys until they got older. She did so until they were about 11 and 12 years old then decided she would look for a teaching position. She had obtained a college degree in French. It was rather late in the year when she decided to look for a teaching job. She sent applications to several schools in the area. One day she got a call from a school principal. He asked her if she could take a position teaching Spanish. She said that she had grown up in Italy and had her college degree in French but had not studied Spanish. The principal said well we are desperate to fill that position perhaps with your background you could wing it, meaning, of course, that she could learn it as she taught it. She took the position and did just that. Later when they moved to the Fort Worth area she quickly found a job as s Spanish teacher and eventually became head of the language department. She then progressed into school administration. After she and Gary returned from the five years they spent in Florence, Italy she got a job as assistant principal of a three thousand student high school near Fort Worth and Gary became a very caring and respected hospital Chaplin. Kevin

Howard Bybee

and Kyle also entered the job market but their process was not quite as complicated and interesting as Jennifer's. Kevin became a very successful dentist with his own dental clinic. Kyle entered the auto mechanic profession in Oklahoma City and has become a first class mechanic. He married Ellen Peterson and she has been an excellent stepmother to his two boys, Evan and Anthony.

ON TRIAL IN ITALY for Preaching the Bible

A DRASTIC CHANGE IN OUR LIVES

As is common to mankind, with the passing of time you get older. By this time in our live Doris and I were far beyond the time for Social Security to kick in. We had been drawing it and were thankful for it because the College church was paying us only $1,500 a month for our work in recruiting *Avanti* workers. Unfortunately we had not done much planning for retirement. As most of you probably know in the past church elders did not even broach the subject of a retirement plan when they talked about salary for an incoming preacher. Fortunately that has begun to change.

During the years we were in Searcy and I was traveling to colleges to recruit *Avanti* workers I had some spare time between trips I began working on a project that would hopefully create some retirement funds. The project consisted of buying small, usually rundown, houses, fixing them up and renting them. After a couple of years I decided to implement an idea I had learned from Paul Buhler, the husband of Doris' sister Marge. He told me that for retirement purposes it is wiser to offer to the renter the possibility of purchasing the house with only $5,000 down and I would carry the note at 8% to 10% interest for fifteen years. We were blessed in that during those years interest rates were high. In time I managed to sell four rent houses on this basis. This gave us some retirement funds. However, at that time we were thinking very little about retirement and made no specific plans in that regard.

We have always known that regardless of what happens if you do your part the Lord will provide. However, we never dreamed that it would be so obvious and so timely. One day our son Kevin called us and said: "Hey, I am getting ready to build a new house, what would think if I decided to build a parent suite onto it?" After we picked ourselves up off the floor and recovered our voices we said, "Yeah! That would be an unexpected blessing." Kevin's plans proceeded in building the house and in 2011 we sold our house in Searcy and much of our furniture and moved to Owasso, OK. It is a very nice small town just seven miles north of Tulsa. Kevin's house is beautiful and is located just five miles east of downtown Owasso in a wooded area. In fact, we occasionally see deer walking through the yard. The parent suite is very nice and adequate for Doris and me. The house is large and that soon proved to be fortunate because a few months after we moved here Kevin got married. You would think that one more person would make little difference but it turned out to be more than one person. Michelle already had two children, Brady, sixteen, and Miranda, twenty. Miranda had a baby from a very troubled marriage. In fact, her husband had proven to be a very unstable, undependable man. They soon divorced and Miranda with the baby, Jaden, moved in with Kevin, Michelle, and Brady. Now the large house is well utilized and we enjoy Kevin's new family.

We were also blessed to find a nice 230 member church of Christ here. It has three very capable spiritual minded elders, an excellent preacher, a youth minister, and a prison minster. It is a very active congregation. It financially supports a program called Hope Harbor that is a Children's Home and Academy which provides on-site services for at-risk teens. The prison minister teaches Bible classes at the prison. He converts and baptizes prisoners regularly. I will not go into all the things the church is involved in but will say that we feel blessed to find such an active congregation of the Lord's church to be part of.

ON TRIAL IN ITALY for Preaching the Bible

NINE MEMBERS OF THIS CONGREGATION ARE PREACHERS

I also found a very nice golf course just three and a half miles from where we live. I have continued to play pretty regularly. I didn't know anyone at first so I just started playing here. As is the case at most golf courses when a single player catches up with a twosome or threesome they will ask him if he would like to join them. That happened a few times and in the process of getting acquainted when the question of age came up and I said I was 87 they usually said something like "wow" I hope I can still play when I am that age. One day I caught up to a man and his son-in-law playing together. They asked me to join them and the older man, Dave who was 70, seemed more impressed than usual at my age and the fact that I am still playing golf. It turned out that he and I played pretty equal scores. When we finished that day he asked me if I would like to play together again and I gladly accepted. That was the beginning of a long period of competition and of an ongoing friendship. He is a very nice guy, an incessant talker but I enjoy that. He says that he is a Christian because when he was born his mother had him baptized by a Congregational preacher with a drop of water onto his head from a rose petal. However, he and his wife do not go to church. He has become an evangelistic target for me and it is ongoing. I have gone about it very slowly and carefully in order not to offend or discourage him. I have sent him a number of Bible studies by email and he seems to appreciate them. However, I have not yet hit paydirt. So far he has not made a move toward obeying the Gospel or going to church. If good works and good deeds could save a person Dave would be saved in a minute. He is involved in an ongoing, extraordinary act of kindness. Early last year he found out that his brother who lived back on the east coast was in serious trouble. His wife had left him and taken most of his savings. His health was not good and he ended up in a very inadequate and poorly run nursing home. Dave drove about 2,500 miles round trip and brought him back to live with him and his wife. They discovered that he is actually bed ridden but they bathe, feed, and care for him. You can see why I said that if works could save Dave would be in good shape but we must have an obedient, working faith. In the postscript below you can see what that is. The apostle Paul says, "We sow the seed and God gives the increase." As I write this I am scheduled to meet Dave tomorrow for a golf game.

THE END

WITH A SPIRITUAL POSTSCRIPT

Well I guess that is about enough for now. I am only 90, so in ten more years I will write a sequel to this. I don't know who all will read this and of those of you who do I do not know where you are or how far along you are on your spiritual journey through this life. You may be firmly and securely in the Lord's hands or you may not yet be there. I want to leave here at the end of my life story an outline of scriptural teaching what is fundamental in showing how to obtain assurance in regard to the eternal salvation of our souls. I want to leave this, first of all, to my children and grandchildren and pray that they will not only read and enjoy these memoirs but that they will also be helped in their journey across the river to that grand reunion beyond the blue.

WOULD YOU LIKE TO KNOW FOR SURE THAT YOU ARE GOING TO HEAVEN?

READ ON

1 John 5:13 *13 These things I have written to you who believe in the name of the Son of God, so that you may **know** that you have eternal life.*

YOU DON'T PAY FOR A GIFT

Ephesians 2:8 *for by grace you have been saved through faith; and that not of yourselves, it is the gift of God*

There's no way we can be good enough.

Luke 17:7-10 *But who is there of you, having a servant plowing or keeping sheep, that will say unto him, when he is come in from the field, Come straightway and sit down to meat; 8 and will not rather say unto him, Make ready wherewith I may sup, and gird thyself, and serve me, till I have eaten and drunken; and afterward thou shalt eat and drink? 9 Does he thank the servant because he did the things that were commanded? 10 Even so you also, when you shall have done all the things that are commanded you, say, we are unprofitable servants; we have done that which it was our duty to do.*

THIS is man's predicament?

Romans 3:10 *as it is written, There is none righteous, no, not one*

Romans 3:23 *for all have sinned, and fall short of the glory of God*

What is sin?

1 John 3:4 *everyone who practices sin also practices lawlessness; and sin is lawlessness.*

1 John 3:4 (New Living Translation)
Everyone who sins is breaking God's law, for all sin is doing what is contrary to the law of God.

WE DON'T ALWAYS DO EVERYTHING RIGHT

Ephesians 4:25 *Therefore, laying aside falsehood, **SPEAK TRUTH** each one of you with his neighbor, for we are members of one another.* [26] ***be angry, and yet do not sin; do not let the sun go down on your anger,*** [27] *and do not give the devil an opportunity.* [28] *He who steals must **steal no longer**; but rather he must labor, performing with his own hands what is good, so that he will have something **to share with one who has** Need.* [29] *Let **no unwholesome word** proceed from your mouth, **but only** such a word as is **good for edification** according to the need of the moment, so that it will give grace to those who hear.* [30] *Do not grieve the Holy Spirit of God, by whom you were sealed for the day of redemption.* [31] *Let all bitterness and wrath and anger and clamor (brawling) and slander be put away from you, along with all malice.*

THE MOST DIFFICULT OF ALL

James 4:17 *Therefore, to one who knows the right thing to do and does not do it, to him it is sin*

James 2:10 *For whoever keeps the whole law and yet stumbles in one point, he has become **guilty of all**.*

IT LOOKS HOPELESS

ON TRIAL IN ITALY for Preaching the Bible

THE JUST CONSEQUENCES OF SIN

Revelation 20:13-15 *the sea gave up the dead which were in it, and (I) death and Hades gave up the dead which were in them; and they were judged, every one of them according to their deeds* **14** *Then death and Hades were thrown into the lake of fire This is the second death, the lake of fire.* **15** *And if anyone's name was not found written in the book of life, he was thrown into* **the lake of fire**

THE GREATEST OF ALL QUESTIONS WAS ASKED BY THE APOSTLE PAUL:

Romans 7:24 *Wretched man that I am!* **Who will set me free from the body of this death?**

WE ARE THANKFUL THAT GOD PROVIDED A SOLUTION

CHRIST DIED THAT SINNERS MIGHT BE SAVED

Romans 3:25-26 *God presented Christ as a sacrifice of atonement, through the shedding of his blood to be received by faith. He did this to demonstrate his righteousness, because in his forbearance he had left the sins committed beforehand unpunished.* **26** *he did it to demonstrate his righteousness at the present time, so as to be* ***just*** *and the one who* ***justifies*** *those who have faith in Jesus.*

Romans 5:8-10 *But God demonstrates His own love toward us, in that while we were yet sinners, Christ died for us.* **9** *Much more then, having now been justified by His blood, we shall be saved from the wrath of God through Him.* **10** *For if while we were enemies we were reconciled to God through the death of His Son, much more, having been reconciled, we shall be saved by His life.*

1 Peter 2:22-24 *who did no sin, neither was guile found in his mouth* ²³ *who, when he was reviled, reviled not again; when he suffered threatened not; but committed himself to him that judges righteously* ²⁴ *who his own self bare our sins in his body upon the tree, that we, having died unto sins, might live unto righteousness; by whose stripes ye were healed.*

Philippians 2:5-11 *Have this mind among yourselves, which is yours in Christ Jesus,* ⁶ *who, though he was in the form of God, did not count equality with God a thing to be grasped,* ⁷ *but made himself nothing, taking the form of a servant, being born in the likeness of men.* ⁸ *And being found in human form, he humbled himself by becoming obedient to the point of death, even death on a cross.* ⁹ *Therefore God has highly exalted him and bestowed on him the name that is above every name,* ¹⁰ *so that at the name of Jesus every knee should bow, in heaven and on earth and under the earth,* ¹¹ *and every tongue confess that Jesus Christ is Lord, to the glory of God the Father.*

Matthew 27:46 *And about the ninth hour Jesus cried out with a loud voice, saying, "Eli, Eli, lema sabachthani?" that is, "My God, my God, why have you forsaken me?"*

WHY DID GOD FORSAKE CHRIST ON THE CROSS?

2 Corinthians 5:21 *For our sake he made him to be sin who knew no sin, so that in him we might become the righteousness of God.*

CHRIST TOOK OUR SINS UPON HIMSELF AND GOD CANNOT ASSOCIATE WITH SIN

Yes Jesus paid the price for our sins and as the verse says *"whoever believes in him* shall not perish but have everlasting life" and Ephesians 2:8 says, *For by grace you have been saved through faith.*

What is important to know is the scriptural definition of faith. It is not just a mental assent, recognizing Jesus as Lord? It is much more than that: As the following scriptures tell us

James 2:19 *You believe that God is one; you do well. Even the demons believe – and shudder!*

**Yes, THE DEMONS <u>BELIEVE</u>,
IN FACT THEY KNOW,
THAT JESUS
IS THE SON OF GOD
BUT THEY DO NOT FOLLOW HIM.**

James 2:26 For as the *body apart from the spirit is dead, so also faith apart from works is dead.*

**FAITH IS DEAD IF IT DOES NOT ACT
BY DOING WHAT THE SCRIPTURE COMMANDS
AND CONSEQUENTLY
IT IS NOT TRUE SCRIPTURAL FAITH.**

John 12:42 *Nevertheless, many even of the authorities believed in him, but for fear of the Pharisees they did not confess it, so that they would not be put out of the synagogue;*

**THE SCRIPTURE SAYS THAT THEY BELIEVED
BUT THEY WERE NOT SAVED
BECAUSE THEIR FAITH
WAS NOT TRUE SCRIPTURAL FAITH.**

Galatians 5:6 *in Christ Jesus neither circumcision nor uncircumcision counts for anything, the only thing that counts is faith <u>working</u> through love.*

TRUE FAITH IS A WORKING FAITH

Romans 1:5 *Through whom we have received grace and apostleship to bring about the <u>obedience</u> of faith for the sake of his name among all the nations,*

TRUE FAITH IS AN OBEDIENT FAITH

How is scriptural faith manifested?

The following scriptures tell us;
Matthew 10:32 *So everyone who <u>confesses me</u> before men, I also will confess before my Father who is in heaven,*
Luke 13:3 *I tell you; but unless you <u>repent</u>, you will all likewise perish.*

Acts 3:19 *<u>Repent</u> and turn again that your sins may be blotted out.*

Matthew 28:18-20 *Jesus came and said to them, "All authority in heaven and on earth has been given to me. ¹⁹ Go therefore and make disciples of all nations, <u>baptizing</u> them in the name of the Father and of the Son and of the Holy Spirit, ²⁰ teaching them to observe all that I have commanded you. And behold, I am with you always, to the end of the age."*

Mark 16:15-16 *he said to them, "Go into all the world and proclaim the gospel to the whole creation. ¹⁶ Whoever believes and is <u>baptized</u> will be saved, but whoever does not believe will be condemned*

John 3:1-5 *Now there was a man of the Pharisees named Nicodemus, a ruler of the Jews. ² This man came to Jesus by night and said to him, "Rabbi, we know that you are a teacher come from God, for no one can do these signs that you do unless God is with him." ³ Jesus answered him, "Truly, truly, I say to you, unless one is born again he cannot see the kingdom of God." ⁴ Nicodemus said to him, "How can a man be born when he is old? Can he enter a second time into his mother's womb and be born?"⁵ Jesus answered, "Truly, truly, I say to you, unless one is <u>born of water and the Spirit</u>, he cannot enter the kingdom of God.*

Acts 2:38 *Peter said to them, "Repent and be <u>baptized</u> every one of you in the name of Jesus Christ <u>for the forgiveness of your sins</u>, and you will receive the gift of the Holy Spirit*

THIS VERSE IS THE CLEAREST ONE IN THE SCRIPTURE TELLING US WHEN OUR SINS ARE FORGIVEN. THE ONLY WAY THAT MAN HAS BEEN ABLE TO MAKE IT SAY SOMETHING DIFFERENT IS TO SAY THAT THE WORD "FOR" IN THE VERSE MEANS "BECAUSE OF".
HOWEVER, NO RECOGNIZED GREEK SCHOLAR WILL AFFIRM THAT THE WORD "for" IN THE GREEK TEXT MEANS "BECAUSE OF". IT IS THE SAME WORD JESUS USES WHEN HE SAYS IN MATTHEW 26:27

'This is my blood of the covenant, which is poured out for many <u>for</u> (to obtain) the forgiveness of sins. – not "because of"

Acts 8:12 *when they believed Philip as he preached good news about the kingdom of God and the name of Jesus Christ, they were baptized, both men and women.*

Acts 8:35-39 *then Philip opened his mouth, and beginning with this Scripture he told him the good news about Jesus.* [36] *And as they were going along the road they came to some water, and the eunuch said, "See, here is water! What prevents me from being baptized?"* [38] *And he commanded the chariot to stop, and they both went down into the water, Philip and the eunuch, and he baptized him.* [39] *And when they came up out of the water, the Spirit of the Lord carried Philip away, and the eunuch saw him no more, and went on his way rejoicing.*

What does the word "Baptism" mean in the original language of the New Testament written by the Apostles?

The original meaning is "immersion". I don't want you to take my word for it so you can check it out in any Greek/English lexicon.

Also by looking at the way the word is used in the verses we have read the meaning becomes obvious.

John 3:5 *"born of water and the Spirit,"* **Acts 8:38** *"they both went down into the water* ³⁹ *and when they came up out of the water,* **Acts 22:16** *"wash away* your *sins"* **Romans 6:4** *"We were buried therefore with him by baptism into death"*

Many scriptures make that obvious:

Acts 22:16 *and now why do you wait? Rise and be baptized and wash away your sins, calling on his name.'*

1 Peter 3:21 *Baptism, which corresponds to this, now saves you, not as a removal of dirt from the body but as an appeal to God for a good conscience, through the resurrection of Jesus Christ,*

Romans 6:3-6 *Do you not know that all of us who have been baptized into Christ Jesus were baptized into his death?* ⁴ *We were buried therefore with him by baptism into death, in order that, just as Christ was raised from the dead by the glory of the Father, we too might walk in newness of life.* ⁵ *For if we have been united with him in a death like his, we shall certainly be united with him in a resurrection like his.* ⁶ *We know that our old self was crucified with him in order that the body of sin might be brought to nothing, so that we would no longer be enslaved to sin.*

THE GOSPEL

2 Thessalonians 1:8 He *will punish those who do not know God and do not obey the gospel of our Lord Jesus.*

INTERESTINGLY, NOT KNOWING GOD AND NOT OBEYING THE GOSPEL HAVE THE SAME CONSEQUENCES

As we are studying the scripture to find out how we can know that we are saved we have seen that we **must believe that Jesus is the Christ, we must confess that with our mouth, we must repent of our sins and we must be baptized by immersion for the forgiveness of our sins.** The verse just above (2 Thessalonians 1:8) also connects the process of becoming a Christian to obeying the gospel.

WHAT DOES IT MEAN TO OBEY THE GOSPEL?

The apostle Paul tells us what the Gospel is in God's eyes:
1 Corinthians 15:2-6 *By this **gospel** you are saved, if you hold firmly to the word I preached to you. Otherwise, you have believed in vain.³ For what I received I passed on to you as of first importance: that Christ died for our sins according to the Scriptures, ⁴ that he was buried, that he was raised on the third day according to the Scriptures, ⁵ and that he appeared to Cephas, and then to the Twelve.*

IN OTHER WORDS THE ESSENCE OF THE GOSPEL IS THE DEATH, BURIAL AND RESURRECTION OF JESUS.

Take another look at the scripture we just read in our study about becoming a Christian and see how baptism is clearly the final step in that process:

Romans 6:3-6 *Do you not know that all of us who have been baptized into Christ Jesus were baptized into his* **death***?* ⁴ *We were* **buried** *therefore with him by baptism into death, in order that, just as Christ was* **raised** *from the dead by the glory of the Father, we too might walk in newness of life.* ⁵ *For if we have been united with him in a death like his, we shall certainly be united with him in a resurrection like his.*

Therefore it becomes obvious that obeying the gospel **is** becoming a Christian by believing in Jesus (**Mk. 16:16**), repenting of our sins (**Lk. 13:3**), confessing Jesus as the Christ the Son of God (**Rom. 10:19**) and being immersed in baptism for the remission of our sins.

Clearly the Lord wanted us to become Christians by experiencing a heartfelt faith and reenacting with our bodies what He did for us. That, as you can see, is what he says in verse 5 of Romans 6: "*For if we have been united with him in a death like his, we shall certainly be united with him in a resurrection like his.*"

This means, of course, that if a person is immersed for any reason other than to bury the old man of sin and come forth to a new life in Christ he has not obeyed the gospel and his soul is in jeopardy. The purpose for which we do anything is central to or can be even more important than the act itself. If a person were baptized in the name of Allah, thinking that was just another name of God, he would, of course want to correct that by being baptized in the right name and for the right reason.

Galatians 3:27 *For as many of you as were baptized into Christ have put on Christ.*

Galatians 2:20 *I have been crucified with Christ. It is no longer I who live, but Christ who lives in me. And the life I now live in the flesh I live by faith in the Son of God, who loved me and gave himself for me.*

The scripture that we began with, as you know, says: **1 John 5:13** *These things I have written to you who believe in the name of the Son of God, so that you may* **know** *that you have eternal life.*

ON TRIAL IN ITALY for Preaching the Bible

The Holy Spirit guided the Apostles in writing the New Testament; therefore it is God's word to tell us how to be saved. The scriptures we have read tell us how to become Christians, how to inter into communion with Christ, how to be saved. We want to make sure we have followed God's will in this regard, **in Becoming a Christian**, Of course, this is just the beginning.

When we arise from the waters of baptism WE ARE IN Christ, He is in **us:** Romans 8:10 But if **Christ** is **in you**, then even though **your** body is subject to death because of sin, the Spirit gives life because of righteousness.

When we become Christians we must begin as best we can to follow the Lord's will.

Colossians 3:1 *If then you have been raised with Christ, seek the things that are above, where Christ is, seated at the right hand of God.*

1 John 1:7 *But if we walk in the light, as he is in the light, we have fellowship with one another, and the blood of Jesus his Son cleanses us from all sin.*

TO WALK IN THE LIGHT MEANS THAT YOU STRIVE TO MAINTAIN AN OBEDIENT, WORKING FAITH and that after being baptized you become a part of a church that follows only the Bible, whose worship, organization and activity is in harmony with the church described in the New Testament.

1 Corinthians 4:6 *Now, brothers and sisters, I have applied these things to myself and Apollos for your benefit, so that you may learn from us the meaning of the saying, "Do not go beyond what is written."*

I firmly believe the church of Christ fits that category of not going beyond what is written. Its motto is "we speak where the Bible speaks and are silent where the Bible is silent". In fact its members all believe that the church today should be a mirror of the church of the first century in all the basic elements that are

clearly depicted in the New Testament. The Lord' church is completely autonomous. It has no central organization that makes laws for the whole church. That's the way it should be.

1 John 5:13 *I write these things to you who believe in the name of the Son of God that you may know that you have eternal life.*

**IF YOU HAVE DONE
AND CONTINUE TO DO
THE THINGS TAUGHT IN THESE SCRIPTURES
YOU CAN KNOW YOU WILL BE IN HEAVEN.**

"The LORD bless you and keep you;
[25] the LORD make his face shine on you
and be gracious to you;

Howard Bybee

www.ingramcontent.com/pod-product-compliance
Lightning Source LLC
Chambersburg PA
CBHW060833050426

42453CB00008B/670